MEETING
St. John
TODAY

Understanding the Man,
His Mission, and His Message

DANIEL J. HARRINGTON, SJ

LOYOLA PRESS.
A JESUIT MINISTRY
Chicago

LOYOLA PRESS.
A JESUIT MINISTRY

3441 N. Ashland Avenue
Chicago, Illinois 60657
(800) 621-1008
www.loyolapress.com

Cover picture credit © Mary Evans Picture Library / Alamy

Library of Congress Cataloging-in-Publication Data
Harrington, Daniel J.
  Meeting St. John today : understanding the man, his mission, and his message /
Daniel J. Harrington.
    p. cm.
  ISBN-13: 978-0-8294-2917-6
  ISBN-10: 0-8294-2917-4
  1. John, the Apostle, Saint. 2. Bible. N.T. John--Criticism, interpretation, etc.
3. Bible. N.T. Epistles of John--Criticism, interpretation, etc. 4. Bible. N.T.
Revelation--Criticism, interpretation, etc. I. Title. II. Title: Meeting Saint John
today.
  BS2455.H37 2011
  226.5'06--dc22

178-3897   2010040253
Printed in the United States of America
10 11 12 13 14 15 16 Versa 10 9 8 7 6 5 4 3 2 1

Contents

John—The Evangelist for All Seasons

Since the late second century, John's Gospel has been symbolized by the eagle, presumably because its theological thought soars so very high. It has also been known as the "spiritual" Gospel. That description carries a variety of meanings. John's Gospel presents Jesus in his person and teaching as the revealer and the revelation of God, and so as the foundation of every sound Christian spirituality. Throughout its story of Jesus, this Gospel challenges readers to be on the side of the "spirit" as opposed to that of the "flesh." And it speaks to a community of believers (the church) who are animated and guided by the Holy Spirit.

Unlike the Gospels of Matthew, Mark, and Luke, in the current lectionary of Scripture texts for Sundays there is no separate year dedicated primarily to John's Gospel. Instead, selections from John's Gospel appear most prominently in the seasons of Lent and Easter in all the lectionary cycles, both on Sundays and weekdays. Passages from John are also included in the Christmas season and in Ordinary Time. The idea seems to be that John can and does provide spiritual depth to the most important moments in the liturgical unfolding of Jesus' life, death, and Resurrection.

In the New Testament we meet St. John (who traditionally is identified as John the son of Zebedee) primarily through the Gospel that bears his name. This is probably not the same person who wrote the book of Revelation (also named John) or the three letters in John's name (known as "the Elder"), though there are links between all these writings. Even with John's Gospel we are more likely dealing with a complex tradition, school, or circle that developed over many years than with a single author working entirely on his own. And so the focus of this book is not the biography of John the son of Zebedee (which is not possible anyway). Rather, it is primarily concerned with the distinctive portrait of Jesus that emerges from the late first-century composition that we know today as the "Gospel according to John." In this way we today can best meet the elusive figure we call St. John.

After a brief introduction to the Evangelist and his Gospel, there follows six chapters of narrative analysis of the entire Gospel. These chapters focus on the Gospel's key words and images, characters, plot, literary forms, indications of time and place, and theological message. Next there is a chapter on the historical setting of the Gospel and, in particular, the problem posed by its negative portrayal of the Jews. Then there are two chapters about John's Gospel in church life, one that illustrates the place of this Gospel in the seasons of the church's lectionary, and another that makes correlations between John's Gospel and the Spiritual Exercises of Ignatius of Loyola. Questions for reflection and discussion are provided at the end of each chapter. This book can be used easily by Bible study groups as well as by individual readers.

I have drawn on material in an earlier work entitled *John's Thought and Theology: An Introduction* (Wilmington, DE: Michael Glazier, 1990). Michael Glazier himself has been a source of great encouragement and friendship to me, and in writing this work I have often thought of him with deep affection. I dedicate this book to him with thanks.

PART ONE

Meeting St. John

And the Word became flesh and lived among us, and we have seen his glory, the glory as of a father's only son, full of grace and truth. . . . From his fullness we have all received, grace upon grace. The law indeed was given through Moses; grace and truth came through Jesus Christ. No one has ever seen God. It is God the only Son, who is close to the Father's heart, who has made him known.

—John 1:14, 16–18

1

The Evangelist
and His Gospel

John's Gospel is different from the others. The Synoptic Gospels—Matthew, Mark, and Luke—provide a "common viewpoint" (synopsis) about Jesus. But apart from the account of Jesus' suffering, death, and Resurrection, almost everything in John's Gospel is absent from the Synoptic Gospels, and vice versa. According to John, much of Jesus' public ministry takes place in Jerusalem and Judea rather than in Galilee. In this Gospel, Jesus' public career spans three Passover celebrations (see 2:13; 6:4; 11:55) and thus three years, instead of one year. John presents a different cast of characters, including Nicodemus, the Samaritan woman, the man born blind, Lazarus, Philip, the beloved disciple, and Thomas. The focus of Jesus' preaching is the revelation of his heavenly Father and his own identity as the definitive revealer of God, while the kingdom of God which is so prominent in the Synoptic Gospels, is in the background. John's Jesus gives long speeches instead of the short units (parables, controversies, proverbs, and so forth) found in the Synoptic Gospels. Jesus (rather than the Jewish Law) is the definitive expression of

God's will for his people. And Jesus' status as the preexistent Son of God, as "I am" and as divine (1:1; 20:28), goes beyond what is said about him in the other Gospels.

Behind John's Gospel

The person named John, who is the subject of this book, is the one we meet through what we call John's Gospel. In the Christian tradition this figure has been identified as John the son of Zebedee, a fisherman who was among the first disciples called by Jesus. He appears in all the lists of apostles, and in Mark 3:17 John and his brother James are called "Sons of Thunder." At several points in the Gospels he appears in the inner circle of Jesus' followers, alongside his brother James and Peter, and at some very important events such as Jesus' transfiguration and his prayer in Gethsemane. Paul places John among the "pillar apostles" at Jerusalem (Galatians 2:9) after Jesus' Resurrection.

However, it is difficult to discern the precise role of John the son of Zebedee in the composition of the Gospel that bears his name. Did he actually write this Gospel as it now stands? Or did he make available his reminiscences of Jesus? Was he something like the patron saint of the distinctive faith community that came to be identified with him and his teachings about Jesus—what scholars now refer to as the Johannine community? Was he the founder of the Johannine school or circle? Unfortunately we can't answer these questions with certainty. Perhaps the most important point of all is that those who produced this Gospel traced their tradition back to the circle of Jesus' first followers, which included John the son of Zebedee.

At several points John's Gospel appeals to the testimony of someone who was close to the earthly Jesus and is called "the one whom Jesus loved" (John 13:23; 19:26; 20:2; 21:7). There are also references to "another disciple" (18:15) and "the other disciple" (20:2, who is further identified as "the one whom Jesus loved"). The reference to "the two disciples" in 1:37 suggests that this person may once have been a follower of John the Baptist. Whether any or all of these figures is John the son of Zebedee is not clear, though it is certainly tempting to view them as one and the same character.

On some historical matters where John's Gospel differs from the other Gospels, John is often correct and so conveys solid historical tradition. For example, it is more likely that Jesus' public ministry lasted for three years rather than one year. Jesus probably did visit Jerusalem more than once. And Jesus may well have been crucified before the Passover festival began, rather than on the first day of the official Passover celebration. Also, many of the geographical references throughout John's Gospel are accurate and suggest some firsthand acquaintance with these places in the Holy Land. There is much sound historical information in this Gospel.

Nevertheless, John's Gospel cannot be taken simply as the eyewitness report of John the son of Zebedee or the beloved disciple. It is better understood as the product of the long reflection on Jesus that was carried on in a distinctively Johannine community for over fifty years and that reached its final form around AD 85 or 90, perhaps at Ephesus. John the son of Zebedee or the one known as the beloved disciple may have been the founder of this school or community in Palestine, which was made up largely of Jewish Christians.

After the destruction of Jerusalem and its temple in AD 70, all Jews (including Christian Jews) had to redefine their Judaism. In this crisis of identity, the exalted claims made by the Johannine Christians about Jesus led to a strained relationship with other Jews and even expulsion from their synagogues. In the late first century, the Gospel in the form much as we have it today took shape. But it represents the literary and theological activity of the Johannine school over many years. It provides both a statement of that community's beliefs about Jesus and a defense against the criticisms made by outsiders. Further developments in the life of the Johannine community can be glimpsed with the help of the Johannine epistles (1, 2, and 3 John).

And so Johannine Christianity began as a movement within Judaism and faced its most severe crisis when its adherents were being expelled from Jewish synagogues in the late first century (see 9:22; 12:42; 16:2). How Jesus fulfilled the Jewish Scriptures is a major concern throughout the Gospel. From chapter 5 on, John's Gospel traces Jesus' activities by reference to major feasts on the Jewish calendar. There is no doubt that Jesus and his first followers were Jews. The Gospel is written in a Semitic style of Greek. As the discovery of the Dead Sea scrolls has shown, its vocabulary and style are not at all foreign to Palestine in the first century. The Johannine Christians probably viewed themselves as practicing a more perfect form of Judaism than their ancestors and rivals did. Non-Jewish observers would have seen the Johannine Christians as a movement within Judaism.

Given the long and complex development of John's Gospel, it is possible and necessary to read it at several different levels. It presents itself first and foremost as the story of Jesus' public ministry and death in the early first century (AD 27–30). But it also uses the stories about Jesus to cast light on the crises faced by the Johannine community in its later history, especially as it separated from the synagogue. These stories were expanded and adapted over the years to provide advice for new situations, just as they have been used in church life throughout the centuries.

As the Dead Sea scrolls and other ancient Jewish texts have shown, many Jews in the first century, while acknowledging the supreme authority of God, divided all present reality into two powers and two camps. The children of light do the deeds of light under the leadership of the Angel of Light. The children of darkness do the deeds of darkness under the leadership of the Prince of Darkness. In the end, at the divine "visitation," the children of light will be vindicated and rewarded, while the children of darkness will be condemned and punished. This Jewish form of dualism found its way into earliest Christianity and received one of its strongest expressions in John's Gospel. There are no shades of gray in dualistic thinking. It is at the root of the many negative comments about "the world" and about "the Jews" in John's Gospel.

In John's Gospel, the chief opponents of Jesus and his followers are identified as "the Jews." They generally appear in a negative way—as Jesus' opponents in debate, as his persecutors, and as the ones who convince Pontius Pilate to have Jesus executed. Because Jesus and John and other early Christians were Jews, these hostile "Jews" do not represent all of Israel; they are a group within Israel.

There seems to be an equation or identification between the opponents of Jesus in the early first century and the opponents of the Johannine community in the late first century. The so-called anti-Jewish elements reflect the situation in which Johannine Christians were being excluded from the synagogues and were engaged in a struggle against "the Jews" who dominated those synagogues and were contesting the Christian claim to be the people of God. For a fuller treatment of these matters, see Chapter 8.

Literary Features

John's Gospel tells the story of Jesus' public ministry: how he gathered disciples, performed "signs" (miracles), taught about God and himself, instructed his disciples on how to carry on the movement he began, was arrested and executed, and appeared to his disciples as alive again. Although this Gospel may not conform to modern definitions of biography, it does measure up to the more flexible standards of ancient biography in which the person's moral significance as an example (good or bad) was central. However, its claim that Jesus as the Son of God was the definitive revealer of God surpassed what other ancient authors wrote about their heroes.

It has become customary to divide John's Gospel into two large parts: the Book of Signs (chapters 1—12), and the Book of Glory (chapters 13—20 [21]). After chapter 1 (which introduces us to who Jesus is), this Gospel in chapters 2—12 traces Jesus' public activities in Galilee and Judea over a three-year period during which Jesus performs miracles ("signs") and gives long discourses about his heavenly Father and his role in revealing him. Next in chapters 13—17, at his Last Supper, Jesus bids his closest followers farewell, and instructs them on how to continue the movement that he has begun. The passion narrative in chapters 18—20 constitutes the "hour" of Jesus in which his apparent defeat issuing in his arrest, suffering, and death is transformed into a triumph through his Resurrection, exaltation, and return to his heavenly Father. Chapter 21, which may be a later addition to the Gospel, provides another Resurrection appearance and ties up some loose ends about the fates of Peter and the beloved disciple.

John's story of Jesus is highly dramatic. His portrait of Jesus makes his hero into an attractive figure, especially when he is played against his disciples and his opponents. The Gospel as a whole has a certain tragic movement as Jesus approaches his death. The individual episodes mix story, dialogue, and teaching to achieve literary variety. Jesus always expresses himself in an elevated way as befits God's Son. He enters into debates and conflicts with "the Jews." Their misunderstandings (and those of his own disciples) allow him to explain and clarify who he is and how he relates to God as his heavenly Father. At the end of each episode, Jesus emerges as both wise and noble.

In the service of his dramatic program, the Evangelist uses various literary devices:

- misunderstanding: someone misses Jesus' point, and he has to explain further
- double meaning: play on words that can mean two things; for example, "again" and "from above" in 3:3–10
- irony: the reader grasps the deeper meaning that eludes the speaker; see 11:50
- chiastic or concentric structures: parallel ideas or terms pivoting around a central notion
- symbolic language: Jesus as the "Lamb of God"
- inclusion: beginning and ending in the same way, as in 1:1 and 20:28 where Jesus is called "God"

Despite the literary skill evident in John's Gospel, there are some peculiar features and apparent inconsistencies. At the end of chapter 5, Jesus is in Jerusalem, but at the beginning of chapter 6, he seems to be in Galilee. After hiding from the crowds in 12:36, Jesus speaks in public again in 12:44. At the end of chapter 14, he commands the disciples, "Rise, let us be on our way" but stays around for three more chapters until 18:1. Much of the content in 13:31—14:31 is repeated in 16:4–33. The Gospel seems to end at 20:30–31, only to start up again in chapter 21 and reach a second conclusion in 21:25.

One way to account for the occasional literary unevenness in this Gospel is to assume that the Evangelist and/or the community behind him incorporated various oral or written sources into the narrative. The prologue seems to contain fragments of an early Christian hymn. The seven major "signs" or miracle stories (2:1–12; 4:46–54; 5:1–9; 6:1–15; 6:16–21; 9:1–7; 11:1–44) may have been taken from an earlier collection. The long speeches, especially the farewell discourses in chapters 13—17, probably were in circulation before the final composition of the Gospel. The passion narrative, though similar at some points to those in the other Gospels, appears to have originated as an independent story, at least in part. The idea that these traditional sources were developed in the Johannine school helps explain some of the awkwardness that remains in the text of John's Gospel.

Theological Significance

Toward the end of John's Gospel, the Evangelist states his reason for writing his story of Jesus: "that you may come to believe [or, may continue to believe] that Jesus is the Messiah, the Son of God, and that through believing you may have life in his name" (20:31). There is some ambiguity in the form of the verb "believe" that leaves unclear whether this Gospel was intended to attract those who did not yet believe in Jesus or to deepen the faith of those who already believed. In either case, the consequence of believing in Jesus as the Messiah and Son of God is the beginning of eternal life.

The basic theological message of John's Gospel is simple and straightforward: Jesus the Son of God reveals the Father. The center of this Gospel is the person and mission of Jesus. He is "the man from heaven" sent by his heavenly Father. His death is not a defeat; rather it is the "hour" of Jesus' glory in which he begins his return to the Father. The Johannine Jesus invites his followers to share in his relationship with his Father—a relationship that is characterized by knowledge, love, unity, and mission. In Jesus' physical absence, the Spirit will animate and guide the community of Jesus' followers until "the last day."

John's Gospel is provocative. Everything in this Gospel challenges the reader to come to a decision about Jesus. What do you think of him? Are you on his side or not? What are you going to do about it? Often by what it does not say, John's Gospel raises other questions about important aspects of Christian life and theology. Since it says little or nothing about the meal at the Last Supper, what was the attitude of the Johannine community about the Eucharist? What kinds of church structures and offices did it have? Since so much emphasis is placed on eternal life as having already begun in the decision for and about Jesus, what are we to expect on the last day?

The Johannine presentation of Jesus, especially as it is expressed in the prologue (1:1–18), has provided terminology and ideas for the greatest Christian theologians throughout the centuries. The doctrinal influence of John's Gospel is especially apparent during the period in which the early church councils made definitions about the person of Jesus largely on the basis of John's Gospel. The declarations that Jesus is divine and thus on a level with the Father and the Holy Spirit were based on texts such as John 1:1 ("the Word was God") and 20:28 ("my Lord and my God"). That Jesus had both a human and a divine nature was rooted in 1:14 ("the Word became flesh"). The preexistence of Jesus is implied in 1:1–2 ("In the beginning was the Word").

The language and ideas in John's Gospel have been (and still are) understood by people of many different cultures and at many different times. There is much in this Gospel that would have appealed to various currents within ancient Judaism: wisdom, apocalyptic, sectarian movements, and so on. Both Jews and non-Jews influenced by Greek culture would also have found much to fascinate them. The first commentator on John's Gospel was a Gnostic named Heracleon in the mid-second century. Other Gnostics made use of John's Gospel in their struggles with orthodox Christians. Christians in many lands today (such as India and China) find in John's Gospel their entry point into the Scriptures.

However, John's Gospel can be a dangerous text. Despite its beauty and nobility, it can be misused. Some groups have used its dualism as an excuse to separate themselves from others and to deny any validity to other religious approaches. Anti–Semites have exploited its negative comments about "the Jews" and applied them to the Jewish people in general and throughout history, including present times. Modern gnostics (the "new age" movement, for example) claim John for themselves when in fact the Johannine community opposed such thinking by insisting that Jesus the Word became a person in space and time (see 1:14). And some theologians have used the Gospel's high spirituality and abstract ideas without attending to it as a whole and reading it in its historical context.

We can avoid these dangers, or at least lessen them, by reading John's Gospel as part of the church's canon (authoritative collection) of Scripture. John is not the only Gospel and not the only approach to Jesus in the New Testament. It must be placed alongside the other Gospels and the other books of the Bible. The present text *as a whole* is the authorized version of John's Gospel. We cannot pick and choose among its sayings to bolster only peculiar positions in theology and practice.

For Reflection and Discussion

What do you hope to gain from your study, reflection, and meditation concerning John's Gospel? Why did you choose to study this particular gospel?

The Gospel of John "uses the stories about Jesus to cast light on the crises faced by the [faith] community in its later history, especially as it separated from the synagogue" (pp. 6–8). When you consider this aspect of the Gospel, how might that change the way you read it?

Does the idea of a Johannine community or school behind this Gospel make sense to you? Why, or why not? How does your own situation and community influence how you understand your faith?

PART TWO

John's Story of Jesus

For God so loved the world that he gave his only Son, so that everyone who believes in him may not perish but may have eternal life.

Indeed, God did not send the Son into the world to condemn the world, but in order that the world might be saved through him.

—John 3:16–17

2

Introducing Jesus

John 1—3

The approach taken in the exposition of John's Gospel that follows is called narrative analysis. It tracks John's story of Jesus with special attention to key words and images, characters and their relationships, structure and plot, and time and place.

The first chapter in John's Gospel is like the overture to a symphony or the preface to a book. Its goal is to prepare readers for a fuller appreciation of Jesus, with particular attention to the many titles applied to him, from the Word of God to the glorious Son of Man. It also develops the theme of meeting Jesus, following him, and sharing in his mission.

The Prologue

John 1:1–18 ("In the beginning was the Word . . ") is the prologue to the Gospel. In a play, a prologue is an introductory speech, often in poetic form, that previews the major themes to be developed. John 1:1–18 is for the most part biblical poetry. It contains short units expressed in parallel clauses, and it proceeds by the association of key words. It anticipates some of the major themes about Jesus that are prominent in the body of the Gospel:

- Jesus is a figure of cosmic significance.
- He is accepted by some and rejected by others.
- His mission is to reveal God as his (and our) heavenly Father.
- He makes those who accept him children of God and capable of sharing his special relationship with God.
- His presence is the definitive manifestation of God's glory.

1:1–5. The first poetic part of the prologue describes Jesus as the Word of God before and in creation. The phrase "in the beginning" recalls the opening words of Genesis, and the designation of Jesus as the "Word" evokes the creative power of God's word in Genesis 1. The idea of Jesus as existing before creation and at creation echoes the descriptions of Wisdom personified in Proverbs 8, Wisdom 7, and Sirach 24. However, John goes beyond the biblical models by declaring that "the Word was God." As the Word of God, Jesus was responsible for life and light, and he prepares us for the struggle between light and darkness that will occupy most of John's Gospel.

1:6–8. The poetry of the prologue is interrupted by a description of John the Baptist. John's role is to testify or bear witness to Jesus as the light. See 1:15, 1:19–42, and 3:22–30 for further developments of John as a witness to Jesus.

1:9–15. The second poetic description of Jesus as the Word of God traces his coming into the world as the light and notes

that many of his own people reject him. Nevertheless, his coming has made it possible for those who accept him to become children of God. His coming is portrayed in 1:14 with two rich metaphors: incarnation ("the Word became flesh"), and tabernacle or divine presence ("lived [literally, tented] among us"). Those who accept him see his glory as God's Son ("full of grace and truth"). John the Baptist not only bears witness to Jesus but also acknowledges his own subordination to Jesus on the grounds of Jesus' existence before creation.

1:16–18. The third and last poetic section further develops Jesus' place in the history of human salvation. Through Jesus we have received a superabundance of God's favor ("grace upon grace"). While God gave Israel the Law through Moses, God has now given "grace and truth" through Jesus. Jesus' task on earth was to reveal God to humanity and so open up the way to the Father. How he fulfilled that mission is the primary topic of John's Gospel.

John the Baptist

1:19–28. John the Baptist testifies about himself in response to a series of questions asked by priests and Levites sent by the Pharisees from Jerusalem. After confirming that he is not the Messiah, Elijah, or "the prophet," John identifies himself in terms of Isaiah 40:3 as the voice crying in the wilderness and preparing the way of the Lord. When asked why he is baptizing at all, John explains his baptism as a preparation for the one who is to come, someone so superior to him that he is not worthy to function as his slave or servant (see Matthew 3:11, Mark 1:7–8, Luke 3:16). The final verse locates the dialogue at "Bethany" (some manuscripts read "Bethabara"), east of the Jordan.

1:29–34. John the Baptist testifies about Jesus "on the next day" (see 1:35, 43) as he sees Jesus coming toward him. He focuses on his baptism of Jesus. While the other Evangelists narrate this event directly, John has John the Baptist look back on it as a past event and draw out its significance for the identity of Jesus. John first identifies Jesus as "the Lamb of God who takes away the sin of the world." This is surely a reference to both the Passover Lamb and the Suffering Servant of Isaiah 53. According to the timeline of John's Gospel, the death of Jesus will coincide with the sacrifice of the Passover lambs in the temple (see 18:28; 19:31, 42). Then John points to Jesus as the one on whom the Holy Spirit came to rest, and as the Son of God, which is the most prominent title for Jesus in John's Gospel.

1:35–42. According to this Gospel, the first disciples of Jesus came from the circle of John the Baptist and on his recommendation. On "the next day" John sees Jesus again, identifies Jesus as "the Lamb of God," and urges two of his disciples to follow Jesus. The question that Jesus puts to these prospective disciples ("What are you looking for?") and his invitation ("Come and see") form a fitting prelude not only to the rest of chapter 1 but also to the whole Gospel. The disciples address Jesus as "Rabbi," which means "Teacher," and thus provide still another title for Jesus. Their encounter with Jesus also introduces the vocabulary of discipleship: seeking, following, seeing, and abiding with Jesus. Just as John's witness brought Andrew to

Jesus, so Andrew brings his brother Simon to Jesus. His call to Simon introduces yet another title for Jesus: "We have found the Messiah." On meeting Simon, Jesus promptly gives him the nickname Peter ("rocky"), presumably on the basis of some personal characteristic. Jesus knows his disciples from the start.

1:43–51. Jesus gathers more disciples in Galilee. The call of Philip is simple ("Follow me"), as in Mark 1:16–20 and 2:14. Philip in turn recruits Nathanael by identifying Jesus as the one about whom Moses and the prophets wrote. When Nathanael balks at following someone from Nazareth, Philip echoes the invitation issued by Jesus in 1:39, "Come and see." Philip, along with Peter and Andrew, is said to have been from Bethsaida, a small fishing village on the northeast corner of the Sea of Galilee. When Jesus demonstrates that he already knew something about Nathanael, the latter proclaims Jesus to be the Son of God and the King of Israel (the Gentile translation of Messiah and the title under which Jesus will be executed). In promising even greater things, Jesus evokes Jacob's dream about the ladder between heaven and earth, and portrays himself as the glorious Son of Man serving as the link between God and humankind.

The many and varied titles applied to Jesus in John 1 provide a clear idea of who he is and why he is important. Having gathered a core of followers, Jesus can now begin his public activity.

2:1–12. Jesus changing water into wine at the wedding feast in Cana of Galilee is described as "the first of his signs." It inaugurates a series of seven signs or miracles, culminating in the restoration of Lazarus to life. These signs reveal the glory of Jesus and point forward to his "hour"—the passion, death,

Resurrection, and exaltation of Jesus taken as one great and glorious event.

The occasion for Jesus' first sign is a wedding celebration to
which Jesus' mother as well as Jesus and his disciples have been
invited. When the wine gives out, the mother of Jesus (she is
never called "Mary" in John's Gospel) approaches him and
simply declares, "They have no wine." Without saying so, she
apparently believes that Jesus can and will do something effective
to mitigate the embarrassment of the bridegroom and his family.
Instead, Jesus seems to rebuff her—"Woman, what concern is
that to you and to me?"—and explains that his hour has not yet
come. Nevertheless, she instructs the servants to do "whatever he
tells you." Jesus relents and instructs the servants to fill six large
jars with water. When the servants bring some of the liquid to
the steward overseeing the banquet, the water has already been
transformed into wine. The steward in turn declares it to be the
very best wine served at the wedding. The sign at Cana points
forward to the hour of Jesus and to the banquet in God's kingdom. The biblical background for this first sign is the prophetic
motif of abundant wine available in the last days (Isaiah 25:6,
Jeremiah 31:12, Amos 9:13–14, etc.) as well as the wine served
at Wisdom's banquet (Proverbs 9:2, 5). The miracle is one of the
"greater things" that Jesus promised to Nathanael (1:50), and as a
result, the disciples are strengthened in their belief in Jesus. The
mother of Jesus displays perfect faith in Jesus and so deserves
to be regarded as the mother of all who believe in Jesus (see
19:25–27). After the wedding celebration, Jesus, along with his
family and disciples, goes to Capernaum (on the Sea of Galilee)

and stays there for a few days before going to Jerusalem for the Passover festival.

2:13–22. John places Jesus' "cleansing" of the Jerusalem temple early in his ministry (compare Mark 11:15–17), at the first of three Passovers mentioned in this Gospel (see 6:4, 13:1). Connected with the spring agricultural festival of unleavened bread, Passover celebrates ancient Israel's liberation from slavery in Egypt. It was a pilgrimage festival and attracted many visitors to Jerusalem and its temple. Jesus' prophetic and symbolic cleansing takes place in the area around the places of sacrifice, where merchants sold animals for sacrifices and changed Roman money into the proper coinage. He makes a whip of cords and addresses the merchants directly. His charge is that they are turning the temple area into a marketplace. Later on, after—and in light of—Jesus' death, his disciples interpreted his action as the fulfillment of Psalm 69:9 ("it is zeal for your house that has consumed me"). In his dialogue with "the Jews" about the meaning of his action, Jesus implies that his symbolic dismantling of the temple system is a sign of his own death and Resurrection.

The presence of the Jews as hostile questioners in 2:18–22 and their failure to understand Jesus are typical features of the dialogues in John's Gospel. When they demand a sign, Jesus answers with a saying found elsewhere in the New Testament: "Destroy this temple, and in three days I will raise it up" (see Matthew 26:61, Mark 14:58, Acts 6:14). Only here, however, does the Gospel writer make a direct connection between this statement and Jesus' own death and Resurrection ("the temple of his body"). Only after his Resurrection were his disciples able to understand that he was speaking more about himself than the Jerusalem temple, which had been rebuilt recently as part of a massive project initiated by Herod the Great. Their insight suggests that after the temple's destruction in AD 70 the worship of the God of Israel will be carried on best with reference to Jesus.

2:23–25. Jesus' presence at Jerusalem during the eight-day festival of Passover attracts many who believe in him because of his signs, or miracles. Jesus, however, recognizes that "sign faith" is not always genuine and lasting, and so he keeps his distance from those who display such faith in him. This helps explain the initial coolness that he shows in his dialogue with Nicodemus that follows.

3:1–21. The introduction identifies Nicodemus as a Pharisee and a "leader of the Jews." Nicodemus's coming to Jesus by night suggests that he does not want to be publicly associated with him. What attracts him to Jesus are his signs. He thus represents the superficial kind of faith criticized in 2:23–25. However, later mentions of Nicodemus in 7:50 and 19:39 indicate that eventually he moved to a deeper, more authentic faith.

The dialogue between Jesus and Nicodemus consists of three short exchanges. When Nicodemus suggests that Jesus' signs come from God, Jesus declares that to see the kingdom of God a person must be born *anothen*, a Greek adverb that can mean "from above" or "again." When Nicodemus mistakenly takes *anothen* to mean "again," Jesus explains what he means by "from above." Being born from above (that is, from God) makes it possible to live in the realm of the spirit under the guidance of the Holy Spirit, and to enter the kingdom of

God. When Nicodemus expresses his incomprehension, Jesus expresses his amazement that a teacher in Israel could fail to understand his teaching about living "from above" (from God) and in the spirit/Holy Spirit.

3:11–21. This teaching seems to be a conversation between the Johannine community ("we") and their opponents ("you" plural). Nicodemus disappears, and much of the language in these verses is in the plural form and about Jesus. After contrasting "our" own knowledge and witness with "your" failure to understand heavenly things, "we" point to the descent and ascent of Jesus as the glorious Son of Man, the man from heaven, whose passion, death, Resurrection, and ascension constitute an exaltation that brings salvation to those who believe. Just as Moses saved God's people from death by the lifting up of the bronze serpent in Numbers 21:8–9, so the lifting up of Jesus the Son of Man first on the cross and then at the Resurrection/ascension will make eternal life possible for all who believe in him (3:14–15).

According to 3:16, Jesus' death on the cross was a sign of God's love for humankind, since through faith in Jesus it is possible for everyone to enjoy eternal life. While the word *kosmos* ("world") is often used negatively in John's Gospel, here it is at least neutral and even positive—it is the object of God's love. In Judaism the language of divine judgment and condemnation refers generally to the last judgment, but here judgment occurs in the present with reference to faith in Jesus as the point of decision (*krisis*). Using the imagery of light and darkness, John insists that God's judgment (with the appropriate rewards and punishments) has already taken place through Jesus the Son of God.

3:22–30. John the Baptist's initial witness (1:19–36) introduced and identified Jesus; now his final witness prepares for his own departure and stresses his role as subordinate to Jesus. This passage begins by noting that both Jesus and John were exercising a ministry of baptism. Only John's Gospel mentions that Jesus was baptizing in the Judean countryside (but see 4:2). The scene for John's final witness to Jesus is set by his disciples' report to him that Jesus too is baptizing and "all are going to him." In response, John claims that Jesus' growing popularity does not disturb him since it is God's will, since he himself already admitted that he was not the Messiah, and since he was sent to prepare the way for Jesus as the Messiah. John goes on to compare himself to the best man at a wedding, someone whose task is not to compete with the bridegroom but rather to oversee the preparations and make sure that all goes smoothly. Finally, John declares that it is God's will that Jesus' career should increase and his own should decrease.

3:31–36. While it is possible to take this passage as the continuation of John the Baptist's final witness to Jesus, it is better understood as another commentary from the Johannine school or from the Evangelist (as in 3:11–21). It summarizes key themes in the first three chapters and looks forward to what will follow. It first describes Jesus as the one who is "from above" and "above all"—that is, from God and sharing in God's own sovereignty. Next it identifies Jesus as the witness to God par excellence, even though his witness will be rejected by many and accepted by some. Then it portrays Jesus as sent by God to reveal the will of God and to give the Holy Spirit "without measure." Finally it focuses on the Father's love for the Son and his granting divine authority to the Son, and it repeats the idea that belief in Jesus is the way to gain eternal life.

For Reflection and Discussion

What does "the Word of God" as a title for Jesus mean to you?

In what sense is John the Baptist a witness to Jesus? In what sense are you?

What do the encounters between Jesus and his first followers tell you about discipleship and Christian life?

A Samaritan woman came to draw water, and Jesus said to her, "Give me a drink." . . . The Samaritan woman said to him, "How is it that you, a Jew, ask a drink of me, a woman of Samaria?" . . . Jesus answered her, "If you knew the gift of God, and who it is that is saying to you, 'Give me a drink,' you would have asked him, and he would have given you living water." The woman said to him, "Sir, you have no bucket, and the well is deep. Where do you get that living water? Are you greater than our ancestor Jacob, who gave us the well, and with his sons and his flocks drank from it?" Jesus said to her, "Everyone who drinks of this water will be thirsty again, but those who drink of the water that I will give them will never be thirsty. The water that I will give will become in them a spring of water gushing up to eternal life." The woman said to him, "Sir, give me this water, so that I may never be thirsty or have to keep coming here to draw water."

—John 4:7–15

3

Jesus Powerful in Word and Deed

John 4—6

Jesus' encounter with the Samaritan woman is the first in a series of lengthy episodes in John's account of Jesus' public life. Samaria is the central section of the Holy Land, between Galilee to the north and Judea to the south. There were long-standing tensions between Jews (and Galileans) and Samaritans, as John later acknowledges parenthetically in 4:9 ("Jews do not share things in common with Samaritans"). The introduction explains how Jesus came to pass through Samaria. His apparent success, even outdoing John the Baptist, had aroused jealousy among rival groups such as the Pharisees. The comment that "he had to go through Samaria" suggests that he was thus fulfilling God's will in including Samaritans in his ministry.

4:1–9. The encounter between Jesus and the Samaritan woman occurs at Sychar, a village in or near Shechem, near the land that Jacob had given to his son Joseph (see Genesis 33:18–19). The reference to Jesus being tired is one of the few admissions of his human weakness in John's Gospel. The mention of Jacob's well prepares for the woman's question in 4:12 ("Are you greater than our ancestor Jacob?"). The time is noon, the hottest part of the day, when someone might be especially thirsty. Jesus initiates the conversation by practically demanding a drink from the woman at the well. The disciples are off buying food. The woman identifies Jesus as a Jew and marvels that a Jewish teacher like Jesus would ask a Samaritan woman for a drink of water.

4:10–15. Jesus introduces the concept of living water, and the conversation proceeds with a series of misunderstandings on the woman's part and corrections by Jesus. The woman imagines that Jesus is talking about the living (nonstagnant) water from Jacob's well, but really he is speaking about his own person and teachings that lead to eternal life. Her misunderstanding leads Jesus to contrast the effects of drinking from Jacob's well (being thirsty again) with the effects of drinking from his own living water (eternal life). Again, the woman misunderstands, since she is eager not to have to return regularly to Jacob's well.

4:16–19. Jesus demonstrates remarkably precise knowledge about the Samaritan woman's past and present. She has had five husbands, and the man with whom she is now living is not her husband. This insight leads the woman to declare that Jesus is a prophet. She later moves from this initial statement to the confession that Jesus may be the Messiah (4:29).

4:20–26. Jesus describes the worship "in spirit and truth" that will replace both the Samaritan sanctuary at

Mount Gerizim and the Jerusalem temple. The term "hour" is prominent here, and refers to the time of Jesus' passion, death, Resurrection, and exaltation. While acknowledging that "salvation is from the Jews," Jesus looks forward to the hour when "true worshippers" will worship the Father in spirit and truth. When the woman notes that the Messiah is coming, Jesus identifies himself as such: "I am he, the one who is speaking to you."

4:27–30. When the disciples return from buying food, they are mildly surprised that Jesus is speaking with a Samaritan woman. She leaves the well and goes into the city to tell the people about Jesus as one with remarkable knowledge about her; perhaps he is the Messiah. Her witness will bring other Samaritans directly to Jesus.

4:31–38. Meanwhile, Jesus teaches his disciples about true food, which he defines "to do the will of him who sent me and to complete his work." Then using two proverbs about harvesting—"Four months more, then comes the harvest" and "One sows and another reaps"—he develops the imagery of harvest to represent the full coming of God's kingdom and the importance of those who labor to bear witness to it, as the Samaritan woman has already begun to do.

4:39–45. The Samaritans themselves come to Jesus on the basis of the woman's testimony, and they stay with Jesus for two days. Now many of them come to believe in Jesus not solely because of the woman's testimony but rather because they have seen and heard Jesus directly. Indeed, they proclaim him to be "the Savior of the world."

After spending two days with the Samaritans, Jesus returns to Galilee, where he is well received in light of his actions in Jerusalem at Passover.

4:46–54. Jesus' second sign—the healing of the official's son—takes place in Cana in Galilee, as did the first sign (2:1–12). While in the other Gospels the saying about a prophet being without honor in his own country refers to Nazareth in Galilee (see Matthew 13:57, Mark 6:4, Luke 4:24), in John, Jesus' own country refers to Jerusalem in Judea. The healing of the official's son at a distance—Jesus and the father are in Cana, while the son is in Capernaum—is a variation on similar stories about the healings of the centurion's servant in Matthew 8:5–13 and of the centurion's slave in Luke 7:1–10. When the official begs Jesus to heal his son who is "at the point of death," Jesus suspects that this is another case of "signs" faith: "Unless you see signs and wonders you will not believe." The keyword is "see." When the official persists in his plea, Jesus assures him by word alone that his son will live. The official believes Jesus' word, and on his return home he finds that his son was healed at the very moment when Jesus declared that he would live. By accepting Jesus' word, the official manifests a faith superior to one based on seeing signs and wonders. By reviving the boy who was at point of death, Jesus shows his power over death and his ability to give life, and thus anticipates the seventh and climactic sign of raising Lazarus from the dead in John 11:1–44.

John's account of Jesus' third sign—his healing of a paralyzed man at the Pool of Bethesda (or Bethzatha—the ancient manuscripts differ) in Jerusalem—takes up all of chapter 5, describing the event and the controversy it generates. It also presents Jesus' teaching on his own authority and reflects on the various witnesses to Jesus.

5:1–18. The healing takes place in connection with a pilgrimage festival and at a pool near the temple area that is regarded as a healing center. The description of an angel coming down to stir the waters appears only in late manuscripts and may be based on the paralyzed man's own words in 5:7. We are told that he has been paralyzed for thirty-eight years. So we can easily imagine his response to Jesus' question, "Do you want to be made well?" Instead of directing him to go into the pool, Jesus heals by the power of his word alone: "Stand, up, take your mat and walk" (see also Mark 2:1–12). The man is healed immediately and completely.

The Jews note that the healing has taken place on a Sabbath; in their minds, the man's carrying his mat—and Jesus' command that he do so—violate the Sabbath rest. After thirty-eight years, they reason, the healing could have waited until after the Sabbath. The healed man at first professes ignorance about the identity of his healer, but eventually he encounters Jesus in the temple area and reports back to the Jews that Jesus is the one who made him well. When the Jews accuse Jesus of violating the Sabbath, Jesus argues that since his heavenly Father works on the Sabbath in guiding and sustaining creation, he, too, works on the Sabbath in his healing activity. Now the opponents are concerned not only with Jesus' Sabbath-breaking but even more so with his blasphemous claims that God is his father and that he is equal to God. For John and his readers, however, Jesus' claims are entirely correct.

5:19–30. In defending his authority, Jesus claims that he can and does work on the Sabbath (as God does) to give life and exercise judgment. He begins with a short parable about how a son watches and learns from his father, and then does what his father does. Next he applies the parable to his relationship to his heavenly Father and contends that the Father has entrusted to him the power to give eternal life and to judge who is worthy of that gift, and has made the criterion to be hearing the word of Jesus and believing it to be the word of God. Then Jesus suggests that he will also exercise divine authority in the future at the resurrection of the dead, the Last Judgment, and the assignment of appropriate rewards and punishments. He concludes that in all of this he seeks only to do the will of the one who sent him, that is, his heavenly Father.

5:31–47. So extraordinary are Jesus' claims about his authority that his opponents may need witnesses who testify to the truth of his statements. Thus Jesus invokes as witnesses his heavenly Father, John the Baptist, his own works or signs, and the Scriptures. Then Jesus criticizes the unbelief of his opponents, who fail to accept the testimony of those who bear witness to him. He suggests that their unwillingness to believe him stems from their lack of love for God and their own desire for human praise. According to 5:43–44, they seem more willing to accept teachers or pseudo–messiahs who come in their own name rather than Jesus, who comes in his Father's name. Finally, Jesus points to Moses and the Scriptures as being on his side rather than on their side. They may refuse to accept Jesus out of their imagined loyalty to Moses but, in fact, Moses will eventually accuse them rather than defend them.

Some scholars have argued that John 6 once preceded John 5, since the geographical sequence—Galilee in chapter 4, Jerusalem in chapter 5, and Galilee in chapter 6—seems awkward. Jesus' feeding of five thousand people (6:1–15) sets the stage for his "bread of life" teaching in 6:26–71. The sequence is interrupted by the story of Jesus walking on the water in 6:16–21; see Mark 6:30–52 where these two stories appear in the same order. All four Gospels include the story of Jesus feeding the five thousand: Matthew 14:13–21; Mark 6:30–44; Luke 9:10–17; John 6:1–15. In all four accounts, five thousand men are fed five loaves and two fish, and there is enough left over to fill twelve baskets. There are similar accounts of feeding four thousand people in Matthew 15:32–39 and Mark 8:1–10.

6:1–15. The multiplication of the loaves and fish is the fourth great sign that Jesus performs. John places the feeding of the five thousand near the Sea of Galilee at Passover time and explains that a crowd had gathered there because they had seen the signs that Jesus had been doing for the sick. Unique to John's account are the designation of Philip as the spokesman for the disciples and John's note that a boy was the source of the bread and fish. His specification of the loaves as made of barley evokes the prophet Elisha's feeding of one hundred men with twenty barley loaves in 2 Kings 4:42–44. The description of Jesus taking the loaves and fish, giving thanks, and distributing them provides a Eucharistic dimension to the episode. The crowd's response in declaring that Jesus is "the prophet" (see Deuteronomy 18:18) and in wanting to make him king (the Messiah, or King of the Jews) demonstrates the many facets of Jesus' identity emerging as events unfold.

6:16–25. Jesus' fifth sign—his walking on the water—also appears in Matthew 14:22–33 and in Mark 6:45–52. In all three accounts, the disciples (professional fishermen) find themselves rowing against a strong wind in the Sea of Galilee. Then they see Jesus walking on the water, and he calms their fears by saying, "It is I; do not be afraid." Finally they take him into the boat and head for land. The formula "It is I" is especially significant, since in Exodus 3:14 and Isaiah 41 and 43 God uses similar words to reveal himself, and in John's Gospel, Jesus often uses this phrase to identify himself. Also, by walking on the water, Jesus does what, according to the Old Testament, only God can do (see Job 9:8). The crowd is puzzled that Jesus did not set out with the disciples and yet is no longer on the eastern side of the Sea of Galilee—so they look for Jesus back in Capernaum, on the western shore. Thus the stage is set for the bread of life discourse.

6:26–31. In his introduction, Jesus ignores the crowd's question about when and how he got to Capernaum, and he criticizes their materialistic interpretation of his signs, especially his feeding of the five thousand. Then he contrasts the food that perishes with the food that endures to eternal life, and he defines "the work of God" as believing in the one whom God has sent (that is, Jesus). In response, the crowd refers to the manna in wilderness (Exodus 16) as a sign from God, and quotes Psalm 78:24 ("He gave them bread from heaven to eat"; see also Exodus 16:4–5 and Numbers 11:7–9).

6:32–59. Each of the three parts in this central section proceeds in a threefold pattern: 1) Jesus' statement about

God's or his saving action, 2) the crowd's misunderstanding or rejection of it, and 3) Jesus' instruction about how best to gain salvation. In the first part (6:32–36) Jesus insists that God, not Moses, gave the bread from heaven. When the crowd wants this bread always, Jesus identifies himself as the bread from heaven. In the second part (6:37–47) Jesus defines his task as bringing those whom God has given him to eternal life in the fullness of the kingdom of God. When the Jews fail to understand about Jesus' true origins, Jesus insists that he is from God and has seen God, and that his mission is to lead those who believe in him to eternal life. In the third part (6:48–58) Jesus identifies himself as the bread of life and contrasts the effects of the manna (eventual death) with the bread of life (eternal life). When the Jews assume that he must be talking about some kind of cannibalism, Jesus first relates this bread to his sacrificial death and then seems to allude to the necessity of eating his flesh and drinking his blood in the context of the Eucharist—which is what early Christians did.

6:60–71. These are shocking claims, and John describes the mixed responses they receive even within the circle of Jesus' disciples. On the one hand, some complain that Jesus' teaching is too hard for them to accept. Jesus recognizes that such followers do not believe him and that one (Judas) will eventually betray him. On the other hand, Simon Peter issues the perfect expression of faith put forth in John's Gospel: "Lord, to whom can we go? You have the words of eternal life. We have come to believe and know that you are the Holy One of God."

For Reflection and Discussion

How does the Samaritan woman grow in faith and become a missionary to her people?

Jesus names his heavenly Father, John the Baptist, his own works or signs, and the Scriptures as witnesses to his authority. He refers to himself as the son who does what the Father is doing (for example, healing on the Sabbath). Considering these credentials, in what sense is Jesus "equal to God"?

How might Jesus' bread of life discourse deepen your appreciation of the Eucharist?

4

More Words and Deeds
of Jesus

John 7—9

Along with Passover and Weeks (Pentecost), Tabernacles (or Booths) was one of the three major pilgrimage feasts in Judaism. Lasting eight days in the early fall, it was originally an agricultural or harvest festival. Because the fall harvest demanded a large number of workers who would give all their time and energy to the harvest, they would camp out and sleep in tents, or booths, at night so as not to waste time travelling back and forth to the fields. The regulations for celebrating the feast appear in Leviticus 23:33–36, 39–43. The events described in John 7 take place before the festival (7:1–13), in the middle of it (7:14–36), and on its last day (7:37–52).

7:1–13. Before the festival, Jesus is active in Galilee and avoids Jerusalem because the Jews there want to kill him (see 5:18). When his "brothers" (siblings, step-brothers, or relatives of some sort) encourage him to go with them on pilgrimage to Jerusalem as an opportunity for him to enhance his public

Then Jesus said to the Jews who had believed in him, "If you continue in my word, you are truly my disciples; and you will know the truth, and the truth will make you free." They answered him, "We are descendants of Abraham and have never been slaves to anyone. What do you mean by saying, 'You will be made free'?"

Jesus answered them, "Very truly, I tell you, everyone who commits sin is a slave to sin. The slave does not have a permanent place in the household; the son has a place there forever. So if the Son makes you free, you will be free indeed."

—John 8:31–36

reputation, Jesus resists on the grounds that "my time has not yet come." His time will come in the following spring, at the Passover festival. However, after his brothers have already gone, Jesus changes his plans and decides to go to Jerusalem in secret. Among the Jews in Jerusalem there is some anticipation about his presence and a division of opinions, with some regarding him as "a good man" and others dismissing him as a deceiver.

In the middle of the festival, Jesus enters into dialogue with the Jews about where he got his learning, where he came from, and where he is going.

7:14–24. Jesus explains that he received his learning not from any human teacher but from the one who sent him, his heavenly Father. In responding to the charge that he is a Sabbath breaker (see 5:1–18), Jesus makes a scriptural argument. According to Scripture (Genesis 17:12, Leviticus 12:3), a male child is to be circumcised on the eighth day after his birth. This ritual was observed faithfully even if the eighth day fell on the Sabbath. That means that circumcision overrides the Sabbath rest. If this exception pertains to one part of the person, that which pertains to the health of the whole person can surely be carried out on the Sabbath.

7:25–36. Jesus affirms that he is from God. The Jews mistakenly assume that he is from Nazareth, and so rule out the possibility that he could be the Messiah, since "no one will know where" the Messiah is from. Jesus asserts that he is going back to "him who sent me" (his heavenly Father), to a place where his opponents will not be able to find him. The Jews again misunderstand Jesus and assume that he must be going outside the land of Israel, into the "Dispersion among the Greeks"—that is, to groups of Jews living outside Palestine.

7:37–52. On the last and greatest day of the eight-day festival of Tabernacles, Jesus issues a public statement that creates division within the crowd and evokes even greater hostility among the chief priests and Pharisees. Tabernacles took place in the fall of the year, at the beginning of the rainy season in Jerusalem and the surrounding area, which came after six months of dry weather. The motif of water is prominent in the celebration of Tabernacles. And so Jesus' promise to give water to the thirsty who come to believe in him is appropriate to the festival and the season of the year. The precise origin of the Scripture quotation is disputed (perhaps Isaiah 55:1–3 or Ezekiel 47:1–11), as is the referent of "within him" (the believer or Jesus). In 7:39 the Gospel writer offers an interpretation that connects the living water offered by Jesus (see John 4:10, 11, 14) with the gift of the Holy Spirit in connection with Jesus' death and Resurrection (20:22).

While some in the crowd regard Jesus as "the prophet" or the Messiah, others dismiss their claims on the grounds that the Messiah cannot be from Galilee but rather must be descended from David and must come from Bethlehem. The double irony is that, according to the other Gospels, Jesus is a descendant of David and does come from Bethlehem, and that (according to John) he really is from his heavenly Father. Meanwhile, the chief priests and Pharisees suggest that the guards they sent out to arrest Jesus have been deceived by him, and they dismiss the popular enthusiasm for him as due to the crowd's ignorance of the Law. When Nicodemus (see 3:1–10) insists on due process for

Jesus, he is rebuffed as a "Galilean" (because of his adherence to Jesus) and is told that prophets do not come from Galilee.

John 7:53—8:11. Bible scholars generally agree that the episode about the woman taken in adultery was not part of the original text of John's Gospel. Its vocabulary, style, and theology differ from the rest of John's Gospel. In some respects it is more like what we find in Luke's Gospel. The story is absent from early Greek manuscripts, and it appears in various places in later manuscripts.

Still, this episode has been considered part of the church's Scripture and is so regarded today and appears in the church's lectionary. Its setting is early in the morning in the temple complex, where Jesus has attracted a crowd and is teaching them. Then some scribes and Pharisees bring to him a woman caught in the act of adultery. According to the law of Moses, the penalty is death by stoning (Leviticus 20:10; Deuteronomy 17:7, 22:22–24). Their intention is to test Jesus to see whether he will abide by the Law or ignore it out of his already well-known teachings about mercy and forgiveness.

Instead of ruling immediately, Jesus delays by writing on the ground with his finger. What exactly he wrote is not stated. However, his directive that only one without sin should throw the first stone suggests that it may have been the sins of the accusers. According to Deuteronomy 19:15–21, those who accuse others must themselves be just. As the accusers walk away, Jesus exercises mercy toward the woman by telling her to go away (since there were no accusers left) but cautions her against continuing in sin (thus reinforcing God's justice).

8:12–20. Jesus makes open declarations about himself and also speaks in his own defense. We are not certain that Jesus made these statements during the feast of Tabernacles. But given that four golden candlesticks were lighted at Tabernacles in the Court of Women (also known as the treasury) at the Jerusalem temple where Jesus was speaking (see 8:20), his declaration "I am the light of the world" would be especially appropriate. The Pharisees object that Jesus' statement is invalid because he is witnessing about himself. Jesus replies by appealing to his heavenly Father as standing behind his own testimony and thus constituting the two witnesses necessary to establish a judicial fact (Numbers 35:30; Deuteronomy 17:6, 19:15), especially in a capital case. When the Pharisees ask who Jesus' father is, he accuses them of not knowing either him or his Father. In a perfect summary of Johannine theology, Jesus says, "If you knew me, you would know my Father also." The only reason Jesus is not arrested for making such claims is that "his hour had not yet come."

John 8:21–59 consists of eight short dialogues in which Jesus makes a statement, the opponents (usually "the Jews") misunderstand it, and Jesus corrects them or gives a further explanation.

- **8:21–23.** Jesus states that he is going away to a place where his opponents cannot find him. The Jews think that he is going to commit suicide. Jesus explains that he is from above (from God) and they are from below (this world), and that is why they cannot understand him.

- **8:24–30.** Jesus states that they will die in their sins unless they believe that "I am he." The Jews want him to finish the sentence, thus showing that they fail to grasp the claim to divinity that "I am" involves. Jesus explains that his divine status will become clear only when he has been "lifted up" (crucified and exalted), and that he is not independent of his heavenly Father.

- **8:31–36.** Jesus claims that believing in him will give them the truth and set them free. The Jews object that as descendants of Abraham they have never been slaves. Jesus explains that those who sin are slaves, and that only the Son of God can make them free.

- **8:37–40.** Jesus affirms that in trying to kill him they are failing to do what they have heard from their father. The Jews respond that their father is Abraham. Jesus explains that they are not doing what Abraham did.

- **8:41–46.** Jesus claims that they are doing what their father does. The Jews answer that God is their father. Jesus responds that if God were their Father they would love and believe him. But in trying to kill Jesus they reveal that their real father is the devil.

- **8:47–50.** Jesus argues that the reason they fail to hear God's words from him is that they are not from God. The Jews retort that he is a Samaritan and has a demon. Jesus answers that he does not have a demon but honors his Father, yet they (the Jews) dishonor him (Jesus).

- **8:51–55.** Jesus promises that those who keep his word will never see death. The Jews respond that in saying such things, Jesus is making himself superior to Abraham. Jesus answers by reaffirming his unity with his heavenly Father, "I know him and I keep his word."

- **8:56–59.** Jesus claims that Abraham would and did rejoice to see his day. The Jews object that Jesus could never have seen Abraham because he lived so long ago. Jesus answers, "Before Abraham was, I am" (see 1:1). That claim to divinity is the last straw, and the Jews pick up stones to kill him, but he hides and then leaves the temple.

Jesus emerges from these dialogues as the Son of God sent by God, the exalted Son of Man, and the one who describes himself as "I am." He can give freedom from sin, identity as the children of Abraham, and eternal life. The Jews appear to be on the side of the devil, this world, sin, death, ignorance, and so forth.

A Healing and Its Repercussions

Jesus' healing of the man born blind is the sixth in the series of seven "signs" in what is often called the Book of Signs: John 1—12. This healing confirms Jesus' claim to be the light of the world. After Jesus heals the man, there is a series of encounters that, almost like scenes of a play, reveal with increasing drama what has happened, who was involved, and what the miracle indicates about Jesus' identity. While the man born blind comes gradually to see who Jesus really is, the Jews and the Pharisees descend gradually into sin and spiritual blindness.

9:1–7. Jesus heals a man who has been blind from birth. When they first encounter the man, the disciples ask Jesus whose sin caused the man's blindness. Jesus dismisses their question and explains that this case of blindness will bear witness to the glory of God and to Jesus as the light of the world. Then he uses a kind of healing ritual: spitting on the ground, making mud with his saliva, spreading it on the man's eyes, and having him wash in the pool of Siloam.

9:8–12. First, the healed man encounters his neighbors. They aren't sure it's the same man who was blind before, but he assures him that he is that man. After identifying his healer as "the man called Jesus," he describes in some detail the healing ritual that Jesus used.

9:13–17. Then the healed man encounters the Pharisees. Only now do we learn that the healing has taken place on the Sabbath. This discovery sets off a debate among the Pharisees about the identity of Jesus. Some claim that since he broke the Sabbath rest, he could not be from God. Others observe that only someone from God could perform such signs. When they ask the man, "What do you say about him? It was your eyes he opened," he states, "He is a prophet," advancing from his neutral statement of before—"the man called Jesus."

9:18–23. The third encounter concerns the Jews and the man's parents. The parents identify the healed man as their son and testify that he was born blind. However, they refuse to identify their son's healer or to explain how he was healed. Their silence stems from fear that they will "be put out of the synagogue" for confessing Jesus as the Messiah.

9:24–34. The fourth encounter is between the Jews and the man who was healed. The Jews first try to get the man to call Jesus a sinner. When he refuses, they insinuate that he is one of Jesus' disciples. When they raise more doubts about Jesus and his origin, the man says that all he knows is that Jesus healed him from his blindness and so has done something that no one else has ever done. And so Jesus must be "from God." They claim that the man is a sinner and throw him out of their presence.

9:35–39. Then Jesus, after hearing that the man had been driven from the synagogue, goes to find him. When Jesus asks the man whether he believes in the Son of Man, the man wants to know who he is. When Jesus identifies himself as the Son of Man, the man calls him "Lord," declares himself a believer, and worships him. The point of the whole story is captured in Jesus' comment in 9:39, "I came into this world for judgment so that those who do not see may see, and those who do see may become blind."

9:40–41. The final encounter features Jesus and the Pharisees. Jesus delivers to them the judgment that while they can see physically, they are steeped in sin and spiritual blindness.

For Reflection and Discussion

What are the links between the Jewish festival of Tabernacles and Jesus' speeches in John 7—8?

Identify the various groups of people who misunderstood Jesus. When he was misunderstood, how did he respond—and so what is the impact of those misunderstandings upon the Gospel as we know it?

Trace the development of the man born blind's faith in Jesus. Are there correlations with your own faith journey?

I am the good shepherd. The good shepherd lays down his life for the sheep. The hired hand, who is not the shepherd and does not own the sheep, sees the wolf coming and leaves the sheep and runs away—and the wolf snatches them and scatters them. . . I am the good shepherd. I know my own and my own know me, just as the Father knows me and I know the Father.

—John 10:11–15

5

The Climax of
Jesus' Public Ministry
John 10—12

Jesus' "good shepherd" discourse in 10:1–21 begins without a clear connection to what precedes it. It consists of a parable that puzzles the audience, explanations of two features within the parable, and further division among "the Jews." The discourse affirms that Jesus knows and loves "his own" enough even to lay down his life for them.

10:1–5. The sheep pen in this parable would have had stone walls and a single gate for entry and exit. The parable first contrasts the thief who climbs over the walls with the shepherd who enters by the gate. Then it describes the shepherd for whom the gatekeeper opens the gate, who calls his own sheep and they respond to him, and who leads his sheep and they follow him because they recognize his voice. No stranger can do what the good shepherd does. The good shepherd knows his sheep, and they know him.

10:6–10. The story told by Jesus is called a "figure of speech," and it seems to need some clarification. What get clarified are the interpretation of the gate and the identity of the good shepherd. Jesus proclaims himself to be the gate. That is, Jesus is the way by which people can be saved and can have abundant (eternal) life.

10:11–18. Jesus identifies himself also as the good shepherd. The good shepherd is willing to risk his own life for the welfare of his sheep, something that a hired hand would not do. Moreover, as the good shepherd, Jesus desires that his sheep might enter into the mutual relationship existing between the Father and the Son. This will happen through Jesus laying down his life for "his own." Then there can be "one flock, one shepherd." The "other sheep" may refer to Jews who had not yet come to believe in Jesus or to Gentiles who might yet come to learn more about Jesus from his apostles. However, after giving his life for others in his passion and death, Jesus will take it up again in his Resurrection and exaltation. By way of conclusion, Jesus insists that he does all this willingly in response to the command from his heavenly Father.

10:19–21. The response of the Jews present is divided. Some dismiss Jesus as possessed by a demon or even crazy, and others point to his signs as coming ultimately from God.

Dialogues with the Jews

Jesus' further dialogues with "the Jews" take place in Jerusalem, at the temple complex, during the "festival of the Dedication" (Hanukkah), in early winter (10:22–23). Hanukkah commemorates the consecration or rededication of the Jerusalem temple to the worship of the God of Israel under Judas Maccabeus in 164 BC, after it had been used as a pagan shrine for about three years.

10:24–31. The first dialogue occurs when the Jews demand that Jesus tell them whether he is the Messiah. Out of exasperation, Jesus points to the works he has done in his Father's name and to the gift of eternal life that he has given to his sheep. Thus he points backward to the good shepherd discourse in 10:1–21 and at the same time evokes the memory of David who was both a shepherd and a king (the ancestor of "the anointed one," or Messiah). Jesus caps off his response by declaring once more, "the Father and I are one." To the Jews this latter claim is blasphemy, and so they seek to kill Jesus by stoning.

10:32–42. In the second dialogue, the Jews charge Jesus with blasphemy "because you, though only a human being, are making yourself God." In response, Jesus quotes Psalm 82:6, where God says to members of the heavenly court, "You are gods." The logic seems to be that if God could call angels gods, then Jesus can call himself the Son of God. In describing himself as sanctified by God, Jesus alludes to the festival of Hanukkah, which celebrates the sanctification, or consecration, of the Jerusalem temple. Again he ends the dialogue by affirming that "the Father is in me, and I am in the Father." This time he barely escapes arrest by the Jews and withdraws from Jerusalem to Transjordan where he began his public ministry alongside John the Baptist. Because Jerusalem and Judea are the true home of Jesus according to John, Jesus is indeed a prophet without honor in his native place.

Lazarus Raised from the Dead

The account of Jesus raising Lazarus from the dead is the longest single episode in John's Gospel. It is also the seventh and last of the signs that Jesus performs during his public career (see 2:1–12, 4:46–54, 5:1–9, 6:1–15, 6:16–21, and 9:1–7). It illustrates Jesus' power to give life: "I am the resurrection and the life" (11:25). The irony is that Jesus' ability to give life results in a plot among his opponents to end his life.

11:1–6. The introduction provides information about the main characters. Lazarus lives in Bethany, a village east of Jerusalem. His two sisters, Mary and Martha, also live there. None of them has been mentioned previously in this Gospel, though Mary will appear again in 12:1–8. We are told that Jesus loved all three of them. And yet when informed by a message from the sisters that Lazarus is gravely ill, Jesus does not come to Bethany immediately but stays two more days across the Jordan (see 10:40). The explanation for this apparently peculiar behavior is that Lazarus's illness is "for God's glory, so that the Son of God may be glorified through it." The Johannine Jesus knows beforehand what will happen.

11:7–16. Jesus announces his intention to return to the Jerusalem area, and he explains what has happened to Lazarus. When the disciples try to dissuade him on the grounds that the Jews are trying to kill him, Jesus responds that now is the appropriate time, while the light is still shining (as opposed to the darkness that will set in during his suffering and death). The disciples misunderstand his comment that Lazarus "has fallen asleep" and have to be told plainly that Lazarus is dead and that the purpose of their journey will be "so that you may believe." Thomas's comment, "Let us also go, that we may die with him," not only points forward to the horrible events to come but also ironically prepares for the abandonment of Jesus by the disciples and Thomas's own resistance to believing that Jesus had been restored to life (see 20:24–25).

11:17–27. Jesus' arrival at Bethany and his conversation with Martha establish Lazarus's death and prepare for something spectacular to happen. It was the Jewish custom at that time to bury a person quickly, on the day of death. So when Jesus finally arrives, Lazarus has already been in the tomb for four days. Note that among those consoling the two sisters on their loss are "many of the Jews." When Martha goes out to meet Jesus, she comments that if Jesus had been in Bethany, Lazarus would not have died. We can take this to mean that she believed Jesus could have healed Lazarus. Jesus assures Martha that Lazarus will "rise again." Martha assumes that Jesus is talking about the general resurrection "on the last day." However, Jesus proclaims himself to be the resurrection and the life and defines belief in him as the criterion for enjoying eternal life now and in the age to come. Martha still does not understand entirely and identifies Jesus as "the Messiah, the Son of God" but fails to appreciate all that Jesus is trying to tell her.

11:28–37. Mary goes out to meet Jesus and repeats what Martha said to him in 11:21: "Lord, if you had been here, my brother would not have died." Now the Jews who had been consoling the sisters become witnesses to the events that are about to happen. They see Mary weeping in her encounter with Jesus, witness Jesus' own emotional attachment, and comment, "See how he loved him [Lazarus]!" However, some of them observe that since Jesus had the power to heal the man born blind (see 9:1–7), perhaps he could also have prevented Lazarus from dying. The effect of this section is to highlight Jesus' emotional engagement with Lazarus and the sisters (an unusual feature in John's Gospel) and to heighten the suspense regarding what is going to take place.

We can imagine the tomb of Lazarus (much like that of Jesus in 20:1–10) as a large burial cave in which the corpse would be stored for a year or so, after which the bones would be gathered and placed in a stone container—an ossuary, or "bone-box."

11:38–44. The final section describes Lazarus's resurrection. The large stone is removed. Martha realistically objects because after four days the body would already be stinking with decay. Jesus prays aloud to his heavenly Father, then restores Lazarus to life. The resuscitation of Lazarus is a sign pointing to the resurrection of Jesus and his power to give eternal life to others. However, it is only a sign since it is assumed that Lazarus will again undergo physical death whereas Jesus will not. The description of the stone before the tomb and the burial clothes worn by Lazarus also point forward to the empty-tomb story in 20:1–10.

11:45–57. It is yet another case of Johannine irony that Jesus restoring Lazarus to life should become the occasion for others to plot Jesus' death. The reaction among the Jews to this sign is once more divided (see 7:12–13, 7:43, 10:19), with some coming to believe in him and others reporting him to the

Pharisees as posing a threat. At the meeting of the Jewish council, some members express the fear that if nothing is done about Jesus, the Romans will come and destroy the Jerusalem temple and the nation of Israel (which is what will indeed happen in AD 70). Caiaphas (the Jewish high priest from AD 18 to 36) proposes that one man (Jesus) should die as a way of saving the whole people from the Roman threat. The irony, of course, is that in the eyes of John the Evangelist and the early Christians this is what has occurred through Jesus' death on the cross. The saving effects of Jesus' death pertain not only to the Jewish nation but also to "the dispersed children of God." And so the decision taken by the Jewish leaders is to put Jesus to death. And so once more (see 10:40) Jesus withdraws, this time to Ephraim, a town twelve miles northeast of Jerusalem. As the third Passover in Jesus' public ministry approaches, people speculate whether Jesus will make the pilgrimage; in the meantime, the chief priests and Pharisees send out the order that Jesus be turned in and arrested. The "hour" of Jesus is drawing near.

The Beginning of the End

12:1–19. The accounts of the anointing of Jesus and his entry into Jerusalem are framed by three short passages referring to Lazarus. As Passover approaches, Jesus comes to the home of Lazarus and his sisters in Bethany. The fact that Lazarus is at the table with Jesus indicates that he has really been restored to life. The account of the anointing in 12:3–8 has some features in common with other Gospel accounts (Matthew 26:6–13, Mark

14:3–9, Luke 7:36–50). However, only here is the woman who does the anointing identified as Mary of Bethany. Given that Jesus has already been condemned to death (see 11:53, 57), her action has obvious symbolic value in preparing Jesus' body for burial. Her generosity and enthusiasm stand in sharp contrast to the venal attitude displayed by Judas. While advocating concern for the poor, Judas is also fleeing from the idea of Jesus as a suffering Messiah. Among the Evangelists, only John charges Judas with stealing from the common purse of Jesus and his disciples. According to 12:9–11, Lazarus had become a topic of general curiosity since being raised from the dead. And so the chief priests plan to put him to death too, since many Jews had come to believe in Jesus because of him.

In John's account, the anointing precedes Jesus' entry into Jerusalem. As in the other Gospels, Jesus is greeted by a crowd who shouts out the greeting used for pilgrims (Psalm 118:26–27), and Jesus rides on a young donkey and thus fulfills the role of the humble Messiah in Zechariah 9:9. What is distinctive of the Johannine account and most important is the emphasis on Jesus as the "King of Israel" and the disciples' failure to understand the significance of the event until after Jesus' Resurrection. The final notice about Lazarus (12:17–19) again suggests a link between the great sign of John 11:1–44 and the fact that many people wanted to see Jesus for themselves. The Pharisees' comment ("the world has gone after him") is yet another Johannine irony pointing toward the universal significance of Jesus and the church's universal mission. The various episodes in this entire passage set the stage for the story of Jesus' suffering and death.

The anointing prepares Jesus' body for burial, and the entry into Jerusalem identifies Jesus as the King of Israel. And the mentions of Lazarus highlight that, by giving life back to Lazarus, Jesus contributes to his own death.

More Discussions

The rest of John 12 brings Jesus' public ministry to a conclusion. Jesus engages in dialogue first with some Greeks and then with the crowd. Next the Evangelist explains why the Jews refuse to believe in Jesus. Finally, Jesus summarizes what he has taught thus far about his person and mission.

12:20–33. Jesus speaks to "some Greeks," who are more likely Greek-speaking Jews from the Diaspora than ethnic Greeks. However, when Jesus starts to speak, they aren't mentioned again, and Jesus launches into what looks more like a monologue. He first proclaims that "the hour has come for the Son of Man to be glorified," and relates it to his suffering and death with various sayings: the grain of wheat that dies and so produces much fruit, losing one's life to save it, and serving Jesus in discipleship. Then in a moment that is reminiscent of the Gethsemane episode (see Mark 14:32–42), Jesus wonders whether he should ask his Father to save him from "this hour." But he quickly affirms that this hour is for the glory of God, an interpretation reaffirmed by the voice from heaven. At "this hour" the world will be judged and the "ruler of this world" (Satan) will be driven out. Jesus goes on to refer to his death as being "lifted up," which both describes his body being raised up on the cross and his being exalted to his heavenly Father while drawing all people to himself.

12:34–36. The crowd objects that on the basis of Scripture (see Psalms 61:6–7, 89:3–4) the Messiah is to remain forever and asks what he means by talking about being lifted up and about the Son of Man. Jesus appeals to the images of light and darkness (see 9:4, 11:9–10), and urges the crowd to accept him as the light and so become children of the light. Thus Jesus ends his public ministry.

12:37–43. The Evangelist tries to explain why not all Jews believed in Jesus despite the many signs he performed. His first explanation is based on two passages from the book of Isaiah. Just as according to Isaiah 53:1 not everyone believed in the Suffering Servant, not everyone believes in Jesus the Servant of God. Likewise, just as according to Isaiah 6:9–10, God willed that not all Israelites would accept the prophet's message, not all of Jesus' contemporaries believe in his preaching. In other words, the mixed reception given to Jesus is related to God's will expressed in the Scriptures. To these biblical arguments, the Evangelist adds in 12:42–43 his belief that the Pharisees were putting pressure on those Jews who believed in Jesus by threatening to put them out of the synagogue (see also 9:22 and 16:2).

12:44–50. Jesus summarizes some of the major points made in the Gospel thus far. No audience is mentioned. He begins by identifying himself as the Father's emissary. Next he refers to himself as the light that comes into the world to save it, and to his word as the criterion for the divine judgment both in the present and at the Last Judgment. Then he returns to the theme of his role as the Father's emissary who opens up the possibility of eternal life. As the revealer and revelation of God, Jesus was sent to make manifest who God is and what God wills for us.

For Reflection and Discussion

How does Jesus' parable of the good shepherd contribute to your understanding of Jesus' life and death?

What are some of the most striking ironies in John 10—12?

Why does Jesus keep talking about his "hour" and being "lifted up"? What does he mean by those terms?

I am the true vine, and my Father is the vinegrower. He removes every branch in me that bears no fruit. Every branch that bears fruit he prunes to make it bear more fruit. You have already been cleansed by the word that I have spoken to you. Abide in me as I abide in you. Just as the branch cannot bear fruit by itself unless it abides in the vine, neither can you unless you abide in me. I am the vine, you are the branches. Those who abide in me and I in them bear much fruit, because apart from me you can do nothing.

—John 15:1–5

6

Jesus' Farewells to His Disciples

John 13—17

At the end of his public ministry, which has been full of long speeches and spectacular signs, Jesus turns to instructing his disciples at the Last Supper. After setting the scene in chapter 13, Jesus issues a series of farewell discourses, or testaments, in chapters 14—17 that provide interpretations of his death and instructions about how his followers are to carry on his movement when he is no longer physically present among them. Modern scholars often refer to John 13—17 as the testament of Jesus. A testament contains the last words of a departing hero who looks over the past and into the future, and gives advice to those whom he leaves behind on how they are to behave. Testaments frequently conclude with the hero's prayer (as in John 17) on behalf of children, friends, or disciples.

The Last Supper

13:1–3. At last the "hour" of Jesus has come. According to John, Jesus' Last Supper took place twenty-four hours before the beginning (at sunset) of the eight-day Passover festival. According to John's chronology, Jesus died on the next afternoon, when the Passover lambs were being sacrificed in the Jerusalem temple, shortly before the official beginning of the feast. The other Evangelists (following Mark) present the Last Supper as an official Passover meal, whereas John portrays it as a meal with Passover overtones (like having a Christmas party on December 23 or 24). John's chronology in this case is probably more historically accurate. The double focus of John 13 is the nobility of Jesus who lays down his life as an example for his disciples, and the treacherous and obtuse behavior of Judas and Peter.

Jesus' death will be a return to his Father, and it is the ultimate proof of his love for his disciples. By depicting Judas as an instrument of Satan, John places the passion in a cosmic theological context. In verse 3, he also provides a perfect summary of his description of Jesus in the first half of the Gospel: "Jesus, knowing that the Father had given all things into his hands, and that he had come from God and was going to God."

13:4–5. In washing the feet of his disciples, Jesus does what would be expected of a slave or a servant (see Philippians 2:7, "taking the form of a slave"). Since John does not present an account of the meal itself (but see John 6), the foot washing serves as this Gospel's symbolic action that casts light on the meaning of Jesus' death on the cross.

13:6–11. The first interpretation of the foot washing appears in a dialogue with Peter. It challenges Jesus' followers to accept his humble (and even scandalous) death as the saving action in their lives. When Peter resists having Jesus wash his feet, Jesus assures him that he will eventually understand this symbolic action. When Peter insists that Jesus will never wash his feet, Jesus responds that unless he washes Peter's feet, Peter will not share in his saving action. When Peter offers also to have his hands and head washed, Jesus reassures him that what he has done with his feet will be sufficient. By saying that "not all of you are clean," Jesus indicates that he knows that Judas will betray him.

13:12–17. The second interpretation views the foot washing as Jesus' illustration of his ideal of leadership as the loving service of others. If he as their teacher has performed this act of humble service (foot washing, death on the cross) for his circle of disciples, surely they should be willing to do the same for their fellow disciples.

13:18–20. There is another warning about the betrayal of Jesus by Judas, this time as the fulfillment of Psalm 41:9 ("Even my bosom friend . . who ate of my bread, has lifted the heel against me"). The second explanation is rounded off by the saying that whoever receives the disciples of Jesus receives him and his heavenly Father (see Matthew 10:40, Mark 9:37, Luke 9:48, 10:16).

The rest of John 13 consists of Jesus' prophecy about his betrayal by Judas, his teachings about his glorification and the new commandment of love, and his prophecy about Peter's denial. Jesus' prophecy about Judas's betrayal is given even more attention than in the other Gospels.

13:21–30. John's account of this evening is unique in that it includes Jesus' conversation with the disciple "whom Jesus loved." This beloved disciple will appear again at the cross (19:26–27), at the empty tomb (20:2), and in the Galilean appearances of the risen Jesus (21:7, 20). Only he seems to learn the identity of Jesus' betrayer when Jesus gives to Judas a piece of bread. As in John 13:2, John traces Judas's betrayal to Satan having entered into him. The other disciples seem to miss the point and imagine that Judas departs to do some business on their behalf. John's solemn comment at the end of 13:30 ("And it was night") captures the enormity of Judas's betrayal.

13:31–35. After Jesus' prophecy of Judas' betrayal, Jesus interprets the meaning of his death as a glorification and explains how practice of the love commandment will enable his movement to continue and flourish. Despite appearances, Jesus' death and Resurrection will glorify himself as the Son of Man and of his Father. At last his enigmatic sayings to the Jews about his going away (7:33, 8:21) become clear. They refer to his return to his Father as the climax of his exaltation through his passion, death, Resurrection, and Ascension.

The time of his physical presence among the disciples is drawing to an end. The love command will help keep alive the memory and spirit of Jesus: "Just as I have loved you, you also should love one another." Love should be the sign of the community of Jesus.

13:36–38. Jesus' prophecy about Peter looks back to the case of Judas in 13:21–30 and forward to the account of Peter's

denials in 18:15–18 and 18:25–27. Peter remains puzzled about where Jesus is going. When told that he cannot come yet, Peter protests that he is willing to die for Jesus. In response Jesus prophesies that on this very night Peter will deny knowing Jesus three times. It appears that Peter has still not learned the lesson of the foot washing—that he must accept the gift of salvation on Jesus' terms (the cross) and in God's time (the "hour" of Jesus).

Jesus Says Good-bye

With chapter 14, John's Gospel begins a series of farewell discourses, or testaments, that extend through chapter 17. They serve the same basic function as the eschatological discourses in the Synoptic Gospels (Matthew 24—25, Mark 13, Luke 21) do in telling about the future, when the earthly Jesus is no longer present among his disciples. But the farewells in John are concerned more with the immediate and continuing future than with the end of human history and the full coming of God's kingdom.

In literary form, John 14 carries on the pattern set in chapter 13. Jesus' somewhat obscure statements are misunderstood by his disciples, and their questions or observations provide the occasion for Jesus to explain himself further. Jesus' statements are mainly assurances to his disciples about the importance of faith and love and promises that the disciples will receive divine help in the absence of the earthly Jesus.

14:1–11. In assuring his followers, Jesus urges them to "believe in God, believe also in me," which are effectively the same thing since Jesus is the one who reveals the Father. Jesus assures the disciples that they will have a place with God ("I go to prepare a place for you"), a way to God ("I am the way"), and knowledge of God ("whoever has seen me has seen the Father"). The naive questions from Thomas and Philip set the stage for these assurances, which rest squarely upon the person of Jesus as the mediator and catalyst of relationships between God and humankind.

14:12–14. Jesus promises that those who believe in him will do what he did and even "greater works" (see 1:50, 5:20). He also promises to answer the prayers of those who approach him ("in my name") in prayers of petition. The goal of such prayers and of Jesus' responses to them is "so that the Father may be glorified in the Son."

The second set of assurances features two references to the Paraclete/Advocate, or Holy Spirit. Other major topics are keeping Jesus' commandments and the possibility of life in the future without the earthly Jesus. Those who love Jesus will keep his commandments, which come down to believing in him as the revealer of God and showing love toward God and others.

14:15–17. The first Paraclete passage explains how the disciples will be able to carry on in the future without the presence of the earthly Jesus. The Greek word *parakletos* ("someone called to the side of") can carry the legal sense of defense attorney or spokesman. The "world" (those forces opposed to Jesus and his followers) does not accept the Spirit of truth because it neither sees nor knows the Holy Spirit. Jesus' followers will be given "another Advocate," someone who will stand in for Jesus and continue his work.

14:18–21. While the Spirit of truth guides the community of Jesus' followers in the present, the hope of Jesus' return on "that day" provides them with enough assurance to face the immediate future because they know that their ultimate future is secure. And Jesus grounds the love commandment in a chain of love: "those who love me will be loved by my Father, and I will love them and reveal myself to them."

14:22–26. Jesus clarifies the Advocate's role as teaching the community and reminding it of Jesus' own teaching. When Judas (not Judas Iscariot, see Luke 6:16 and Acts 1:13) asks why Jesus does not reveal himself more publicly to the whole world, Jesus replies somewhat indirectly that the Father and the Son are present wherever love for Jesus and fidelity to his teaching are present. Thus the Holy Spirit will equip the disciples to face new situations while insuring continuity with Jesus' own teaching.

14:27–31. Before departing, Jesus promises his followers the gift of his peace—the wholeness that comes from the eternal life already begun through him and carried on by the Paraclete. He interprets his death as an occasion for joy, since he is returning to his Father whom he declares as "greater than I" because he sent Jesus to reveal him and bear witness to him. His death will also be proof to the world that Jesus is perfectly obedient to and loves the Father. Even though "the ruler of this world" (Satan) is coming, Jesus is both defiant ("he has no power over me") and eager to move into his "hour." The farewell discourse seems to break off with Jesus' command, "Rise, let us be on our way" (14:31). However, there are three more chapters of farewell discourses yet to come in which Jesus continues to instruct his disciples on how to carry on the movement that he has begun.

A Vine and Its Branches

In his second farewell discourse, Jesus emphasizes the love that should prevail within the community of his disciples and warns about the hatred that will be directed toward it from outside. His monologue about love within the community consists of an allegory on the vine and a commentary on abiding in Jesus.

15:1–6. In proclaiming himself to be "the true vine," Jesus appeals not only to the experience of people in the Mediterranean world but also to biblical texts like Psalm 80:8–17, which identifies Israel as God's vine and traces its history from the Exodus to the Exile. The vine passage is called an allegory because each element is equated with some other figure: the vine is Jesus, whose vital power courses through the whole plant and serves as its source of life; the farmer/vine grower is God the Father, who tends to the vine at every stage of its existence; and the branches are those who follow Jesus and so depend on both the vine and the vine grower for their life and care. The vine grower's major activities include cutting away dead branches and pruning live branches so that these might produce even more abundant fruit. The branches either live or die, depending on their capacity to bear fruit, which means abiding in Jesus and keeping his commandments to believe and to love. The vine allegory insists that believers are related to Jesus in a vital way, and that discipleship demands abiding in that relationship and being faithful to it.

15:7–17. The commentary on abiding in Jesus places at the center of this relationship the commandment to love. "Love one another as I have loved you . . so that you may love one another." It roots that love in Jesus' example of perfect love shown by laying down his life for his friends. The disciples of Jesus are his "friends" and have been chosen by him. They exist in a chain of love: "As the Father has loved me, so I have loved you; abide in my love." Their task is to bear fruit, being confident that what they ask in prayer will be granted to them. The goal of Jesus' invitation to abide in him is perfect joy, "so that my joy may be in you and that your joy may be complete."

Jesus' instructions about love within the community is balanced by warnings about hatred from outside the community. The chief enemy is "the world," a term used here negatively to describe those forces that are hostile to Jesus and his Father.

15:18–20. The root of the world's hatred for the disciples is its hatred for Jesus. Since he has taken them out of the world, they no longer belong to it. Therefore they can expect persecution, just as Jesus himself has experienced.

15:21–25. The world hates Jesus and his disciples because it does not know the one who sent Jesus, because it hates the Father, and because it fulfills the Scriptures. ("They hated me without a cause"; see Psalm 35:19 and 69:4.)

15:26–27. However, the community will have the help of the Advocate, who will bear witness to Jesus and empower his

disciples to give witness themselves. In the legal context, the Advocate will serve as the defense attorney and facilitate the testimony of the disciples.

16:1–4. Two examples of the world's hatred for the Christian community are mentioned: expulsion from the synagogue and persecution resulting in death. Jesus offers these warnings so that when they happen, his followers will not fall away. He attributes them to the world's failure to know him and his Father.

Jesus' Departure and Return

Jesus' third farewell discourse reflects on various aspects of his departure and return: why it is good for him to go, sorrow at his departure and joy over his eventual return, and Jesus' use of figurative and plain speech.

16:5–7. Jesus makes the surprising statement that "it is to your advantage that I go away." If he stayed, the Advocate would not come, and the disciples (and we) would be deprived of the fuller revelation and experience of God as Father, Son, and Holy Spirit.

16:8–11. The focus of the Advocate's work is the world, and the Advocate now functions as the prosecuting attorney. The Holy Spirit will convict the world about sin by showing that its refusal to believe in Jesus is the root of sin, about righteousness by showing that the world's unjust condemnation of Jesus will not thwart Jesus' victory as he returns to the Father, and about judgment by showing that Jesus' death will result in the condemnation of Satan as the ruler of this world.

16:12–15. The emphasis is once more on the Holy Spirit's function within the community. The Spirit will extend Jesus' teaching mission by guiding the community in Jesus' way in new circumstances so as to glorify Jesus and his Father. The fidelity of the Spirit is based on the unity that exists among Father, Son, and Holy Spirit.

16:16–24. The second section concerns the disciples' sorrow at Jesus' impending departure and joy at his return. His enigmatic saying ("A little while, and you will no longer see me, and again a little while, and you will see me") throws the disciples into confusion. Jesus tries to soothe their feelings by the analogy of a woman giving birth. While in labor the woman suffers pain and sorrow, but when the child is born these emotions yield to joy. Jesus' promise that in a little while "you will no longer see me" obviously refers to his passion and death. However, the second promise ("again a little while, and you will see me") could refer to his appearances to them after his Resurrection, the extension of his ministry through the Holy Spirit, the disciples' encounter with him after their own deaths, or his return (the Second Coming) at the fullness of God's kingdom. Once more, Jesus urges prayer "in my name" and notes his Father's willingness to grant such requests.

16:25–33. In the third section Jesus admits that he has been using figurative speech, but promises now as his hour draws near to speak plainly about himself and his Father. And so in 16:28 he summarizes clearly what he has been saying throughout John's Gospel: "I came from the Father and have come into the world; again, I am leaving the world and going to the Father." Just when the disciples assert that they now fully understand him, Jesus prophesies that at his arrest they all will desert him and leave him alone to die. Nevertheless, Jesus ends his speech in 16:33 by assuring the disciples of his ultimate victory ("I have conquered the world") and promises them peace in the face of persecution from the world.

Jesus' High Priestly Prayer

Since the sixteenth century, it has been customary to refer to John 17 as Jesus' high priestly prayer, because he intercedes on behalf of his disciples and those who come to believe through them. But a more accurate description is "the prayer of God's Son." In John 17 Jesus prays as the Son of God that his followers may share in his intimate relationship with God as the Father. Jesus prays for himself, for his disciples, and for those who come to believe through them.

17:1–5. Jesus addresses his Father and announces that his hour has finally come. He prays that his hour may be seen for what it truly is: a manifestation of God's glory. Just as in carrying out his work of revealing the Father, Jesus glorified God, now in his hour Jesus prays that he may once more glorify God and that God may glorify him. Thus the reader of John's Gospel is instructed to view what follows in chapter 18—19 not as a tragedy but rather as part of an exaltation or triumph.

17:6–19. Jesus prays for his disciples in a way that portrays them more positively than they appear in the rest of John's Gospel. They are the ones to whom Jesus has revealed God and God's glory, and they have received Jesus' words and have come to know that he was sent by God. Moreover, though they remain in the world, as Jesus' disciples they belong to God and participate in the relationship between the Father and the Son. Jesus prays that "they may be one, as we are one," and that God will protect them from the world and from the evil one. He also prays that they may enter into the chain of mission ("as you have sent me into the world, so I have sent them into the world," 17:18), and that they share in divine holiness and truth.

17:20–26. Finally, Jesus prays for those who will come to believe in him through his disciples. He prays that they all may be one as he and the Father are one so that they may share the divine unity and come to believe that God sent the Son. Caught up in the mystery of the love between the Father and the Son that existed before the creation of the world (see 1:1–2), these believers can come to share in his divine glory, unity, and mission. The Son of God prays that those who believe through his disciples may also become children of God.

For Reflection and Discussion

How might you explain Judas' betrayal of Jesus?

What roles does the Holy Spirit play in keeping alive the movement begun by Jesus?

How would you describe the Johannine understanding of love? How might it shape your own Christian life?

A week later his disciples were again in the house, and Thomas was with them. Although the doors were shut, Jesus came and stood among them and said, "Peace be with you." Then he said to Thomas, "Put your finger here and see my hands. Reach out your hand and put it in my side. Do not doubt but believe." Thomas answered him, "My Lord and my God!" Jesus said to him, "Have you believed because you have seen me? Blessed are those who have not seen and yet have come to believe."

—John 20:26–29

7

The "Hour" of Jesus
John 18—21

There are many parallels and convergences between John's story of Jesus' suffering and death and those in the other Gospels. However, the differences in details and theological perspectives suggest that John wrote independently of them and did not use those texts directly as sources. John begins with the arrest and interrogation of Jesus, and there emphasizes the contrasts between Jesus and his disciples.

18:1–11. The arrest of Jesus takes place in a garden to the east of Jerusalem. During a pilgrimage feast such as Passover, crowds of people would be present. This explains why Judas brought a detachment of soldiers with him, in order that the arrest might occur quickly and without incident. In contrast to Judas's careful plotting, Jesus confidently steps forward and identifies himself by saying, "I am he." The soldiers' reaction indicates that they understood the biblical background of such a statement, and that it suggested Jesus' claim to divinity. Jesus accepts arrest and asks only that his disciples be allowed to go free. His demeanor contrasts with Peter's rash and dangerous act of cutting off the right ear of Malchus, the high priest's slave. Jesus is willing to accept the cup of suffering that awaits him.

18:12–14. After his arrest, Jesus in is taken to the house of Annas for a preliminary interrogation. Annas had been the high priest from AD 9 to 15. His son-in-law, Caiaphas, served as the high priest between AD 18 and 36. According to John 11:49–50, Caiaphas had unwittingly prophesied that it would be better that one man (Jesus) should die for the people than that the Romans should come and destroy their city and their people. According to John's chronology, the arrest took place on the night before the Passover festival began, and the interrogation was preliminary to the actual trial to be conducted by Pontius Pilate, the Roman prefect, or governor, on the day leading up to the beginning of Passover.

18:15–27. John's account of Jesus' interrogation contrasts the cowardice of Peter with the fidelity of Jesus. The distinctive feature of John's account is the appearance of "another disciple" (probably the beloved disciple) whose connections allowed Peter access to Annas's courtyard. Before and after Jesus' interrogation, Peter denies knowing Jesus three times, thus fulfilling Jesus' prophecy in 13:38. Meanwhile, Jesus stands up to Annas and claims that his teaching has been a matter of public knowledge and he is confident that witnesses will exonerate him. As a result, Annas sends Jesus off to the house of his son-in-law, Caiaphas.

The Trial

According to John, the legal proceeding against Jesus took place with Pontius Pilate presiding. Pilate served as the Roman governor, or prefect, of Judea from AD 26 to 36. His headquarters were at Caesarea Maritima, but during pilgrimage festivals such as Passover he would come to Jerusalem to keep the peace. The ancient reports about him portray him as cruel and ruthless, though he was known also to give in to pressure from a crowd.

At the center of John's account of Jesus' trial story is the irony that the one who is mocked as "King of the Jews" really is the King of the Jews to the eyes of faith. While the trial seems to be a defeat for Jesus, it turns out to be a public manifestation and acknowledgment of his real identity. The account is full of ironies, the chief of which is that, despite external appearances, Jesus emerges as the King of the Jews (the Messiah) and the Son of God.

- **18:28–32.** The first scene takes place outside Pilate's headquarters in Jerusalem. The Jews take Jesus from Caiaphas's house to Pilate because they want Jesus to be put to death, but claim that they do not have the power to do so.
- **18:33–38a.** The second scene occurs inside Pilate's headquarters and features a conversation between him and Jesus about Jesus' identity as King of the Jews. If Jesus claims to be a king, he could be executed as a rebel against the Roman Empire. When Jesus explains that his kingship is not an earthly, political kingship and that his real mission is to testify to the truth

(that is, to reveal his heavenly Father), Pilate fails to grasp the nature of Jesus' kingship or the nature of truth.

- **18:38b–40.** In the third scene Pilate goes outside again to the Jews, and declares Jesus to be innocent. Given the choice between granting amnesty to Jesus of Nazareth or to Barabbas the bandit, the crowd prefers Barabbas.

- **19:1–3.** The central scene takes place inside. Pilate has Jesus flogged, probably as part of a plan to release him. The soldiers mock Jesus as a king, complete with a crown of thorns, a purple cloak, and a royal greeting.

- **19:4–8.** In the fifth scene Pilate takes Jesus outside and again declares him to be innocent. However, his plan to release Jesus backfires when the crowd insists that Jesus be crucified. The Jews argue that Jesus should be put to death because he claimed to be the Son of God.

- **19:9–11.** The sixth scene occurs inside Pilate's headquarters and features another conversation between Jesus and Pilate. When Pilate asks, "Where are you from?" Jesus refuses to answer, since the thrust of the whole Gospel has been to argue that Jesus is from his heavenly Father. While Pilate imagines that he has power over Jesus, Jesus as the Son of God has power over Pilate and all earthly political entities.

- **19:12–16.** The seventh and final scene takes place outside, where again the Jews press Pilate to execute Jesus. They argue that if Pilate releases Jesus, he would be "no friend of the emperor." How the Jews obtain from Pilate a death sentence for Jesus is told in great detail, giving the time (noon on the day before the beginning of Passover) and place ("the

Stone Pavement") and allowing readers to envision Pilate sitting on the judge's bench. The dialogue between the Jews and Pilate results in their confession that "we have no king but the emperor," which is a shocking statement in light of their longstanding opposition to foreign domination under Gentile rulers. With this admission, Pilate hands Jesus over to the Jews to be crucified, though clearly it is the Romans who carry out the death sentence (see 19:19, 23).

The Death

John's account of Jesus' death follows a concentric outline similar to the one in the narrative of the trial before Pilate. The center of the passage is the scene of Jesus speaking from the cross to his mother and the beloved disciple. Building up to that scene are passages about the crucifixion of Jesus, the Jews' request, and scriptural fulfillment. On the other side there are passages about scriptural fulfillment, the Jews' request, and the burial of Jesus. John is especially interested in Jesus' identity as the King of the Jews and the Lamb of God, and how, even in death, he fulfills God's will as revealed in the Scriptures.

- **19:17–18.** In the first scene, Jesus carries his own cross, arrives at "The Place of the Skull" (Golgotha or Calvary, where criminals were executed), and is crucified with two others (see Isaiah 53:12). Like the other Evangelists, John does not dwell on the physical torments of crucifixion (which were great).

- **19:19–22.** In the second scene, the Jews request that Pilate change the charge against Jesus that was affixed to the cross to read, "This man said, 'I am the King of the Jews.'" Pilate refuses their request, apparently out of scorn.

- **19:23–24.** The third scene has the soldiers dividing Jesus' clothes into four parts and casting lots for his tunic, thus fulfilling Psalm 22:18—part of the lament of the righteous sufferer.

- **19:25–27.** The central passage features the mother of Jesus, some other women (including Mary Magdalene), and the beloved disciple at the foot of the cross. Speaking from the cross, Jesus commends his mother to the beloved disciple, and the beloved disciple to his mother.

- **19:28–30.** In the fifth scene, with his cry "I am thirsty," Jesus fulfills either Psalm 22:15 or Psalm 69:21 (or both). According to John's chronology, Jesus dies when the Passover lambs were being sacrificed in the temple. His last words, "It is finished," carry the nuance of his having fulfilled the mission entrusted to him by his heavenly Father and having fulfilled the Scriptures. That Jesus "gave up his spirit" can be understood as describing the death of Jesus (taking his last breath) and/or his bestowal of the Holy Spirit at the moment of his death.

- **19:31–37.** In the sixth scene, the Jews request that the legs of the crucified men be broken and their bodies be removed before the Sabbath of Passover might begin. That Jesus really died is proved by the soldiers' refusal to break his legs (see Exodus 12:46), the piercing of his side (see Zechariah 12:10), and the testimony of the eyewitness, who might be the beloved disciple.

- **19:38–42.** The seventh and last scene, the burial of Jesus, is carried out by Joseph of Arimathea and Nicodemus. While both are identified as secret followers of Jesus, their actions in preparing Jesus' corpse for burial suggest that they had not yet understood Jesus' proclamation of himself, "I am the resurrection and the life" (11:25).

The Resurrection

John, like other early Christians, believed that on Easter, Jesus was raised from the dead. In chapter 20 he traces the origin and development of Easter faith in four phases:

- Peter and the beloved disciple find Jesus' tomb empty
- the risen Jesus appears to Mary Magdalene
- he appears to his disciples on Easter afternoon
- and he appears to Thomas and the other disciples.

In these stories the followers of Jesus pass from doubt to faith and from confusion to confession.

20:1–10. John's account of the empty tomb features three characters already familiar to the reader. Mary Magdalene, who had witnessed Jesus' death and burial, goes to Jesus' tomb on Easter Sunday morning and finds it empty. She supposes that the corpse has been stolen and the tomb robbed. Peter and "the other disciple" (the beloved disciple) race to the tomb, and they too find it empty. They enter the tomb and both see Jesus' burial cloths. While Peter draws no conclusion, the beloved disciple is apparently intrigued by the neat disposition of the burial cloths (see 11:44). And so he believed. What did he believe? Presumably it was that Jesus had been raised from the dead. This, of course, would have been a surprising deduction, since resurrection was understood to be a communal, end-time event.

20:11–18. The appearance of the risen Jesus to Mary Magdalene links the empty tomb and the series of appearances in John 20—21. Mary takes another look at the tomb, sees two angels, and tells them that she thinks that Jesus' body has been stolen. Even when Jesus encounters her, she still fails to recognize him and imagines that he is the gardener. Only when Jesus calls her by name does she realize who the mysterious stranger is and what has happened. John highlights the role of Mary Magdalene by mentioning her as the only woman witness to the empty tomb and making her the sole recipient of the first appearance of the risen Jesus. The precise meaning of Jesus' command to her, "Do not hold on to me," remains a puzzle and an ongoing source of fascination and speculation. Mary's proclamation to the apostles ("I have seen the Lord") has gained for her the title "the apostle to the apostles."

20:19–23. The first appearance to the eleven disciples as a group takes place on Easter Sunday evening. The story stresses both the spiritual dimension of Jesus' resurrected body (he passes through locked doors) and its material dimension (he displays his wounds). He proposes the Father's sending of the Son as the basis and model for his sending the apostles on their mission.

He equips them with the gift of the Holy Spirit and grants them power over sin. Thus his use of the ordinary Jewish greeting "Peace" takes on new meaning. His Easter afternoon appearance is the Johannine equivalent of the Pentecost narrative in Acts 2.

20:24–29. Absent during the first appearance, Thomas not only wants the same experience that the other disciples had but also demands empirical proof that the risen Jesus is also the crucified Jesus. On the following Sunday, the risen Jesus appears again, and this time Thomas is present. Again Jesus enters the house mysteriously, greets the disciples, and proves to Thomas his continuity with the crucified Jesus. When Thomas sees the risen Jesus, his doubts dissolve, and he makes the most perfect profession of faith in Jesus in the entire Gospel, "My Lord and my God" (20:28). Just as John's Gospel began by affirming that "the Word was God," so it climaxes with Thomas proclaiming Jesus as "my Lord and my God." The risen Jesus goes on to suggest how those who do not experience the risen Jesus as the first disciples did can come to believe in Jesus in an even better way—through simple belief, even if it is without seeing: "Blessed are those who have not seen and yet have come to believe."

20:30–31. In the epilogue to the Gospel, the Evangelist explains his purpose in writing: "so that you may come to believe that Jesus is the Messiah, the Son of God, and that through believing you may have life in his name." This statement reminds us of the two central themes of the Gospel: the identity of Jesus as the Messiah and Son of God, and his gift of eternal life to those who believe in him. There is some dispute about the meaning of the verb *believe*. Does it mean "come

to believe," suggesting that the Gospel was written as a missionary document for non-Christians? Or does it mean "continue to
believe," indicating that its purpose was to affirm and deepen the
faith of those who had already come to believe?

An Added Ending

John 21 is often described as an appendix or addition to this
Gospel because John 20:30–31 seems to have been the original
ending. The purpose of John 21 is to tie up loose ends: the fates
of Peter and the beloved disciple, the care of the flock after Jesus'
departure, and the relationship of the Evangelist to the beloved
disciple.

**21:1–14. This ending is introduced by an appearance story
that involves both Peter and the beloved disciple.** This appearance takes place in Galilee, at the Sea of Tiberias (another name
for the Sea of Galilee, based on the name of the large city on its
western shore). Seven of the disciples go fishing but catch nothing.
At daybreak a mysterious stranger (who is the risen Jesus) appears
on the shore and gives them instructions about how to obtain a
large catch of fish (see Luke 5:1–11). By following Jesus' word, they
bring in a huge catch. The beloved disciple is the first to recognize
that the mysterious stranger is the risen Jesus, "It is the Lord!" In
his typical enthusiasm, Simon Peter jumps into the water, presumably to meet the risen Lord. Meanwhile, on shore the risen Jesus
has prepared a meal for the disciples. The total catch amounts
to 153 fish. This number has been explained in many ways: the
sum of all the numbers from one to seventeen, biblical allusions

(Ezekiel 47:10), and gematria (using letters to stand for numbers). Whatever its precise meaning, the number and the untorn net are generally regarded as referring to the church and its mission. The fact that Jesus shares a meal with his followers further develops the material or physical side of his resurrected existence. Also, by sharing a meal of bread and fish by the Sea of Galilee, the risen Jesus does what the earthly Jesus did when he fed the crowd of five thousand in 6:1–14. There may also be a eucharistic dimension to the risen Lord hosting a meal with his disciples.

This appearance story is counted as the third in the series of the disciples' communal encounters with the risen Lord (see 20:19–29). While perhaps a later addition to the Gospel, the narrative in John 21:1–14 fits well with the rest of the Gospel: the setting in Galilee, the presence of the risen Lord, the revelation of Jesus' identity, the prominence of Peter and the beloved disciple, the meal shared with the risen Jesus, and the church's missionary outreach.

21:15–25. The dialogue between the risen Jesus and Peter serves to rehabilitate Peter and designate him as the chief pastor of the flock (the church). Just as in 18:15–18 and 18:25–27, Peter denied even knowing Jesus three times, so in 21:15–17 Peter reaffirms his love for Jesus three times, and three times Jesus appoints him to serve as the shepherd of his flock. The saying about the independence of youth and the constraints of old age in 21:18–19 is interpreted to refer to Peter's fate as a Christian martyr after the pattern of Jesus.

The rest of John 21 seeks to clear up two mysteries surrounding the beloved disciple: his death and its relation to Jesus' second coming, and his role in the composition of John's Gospel. There was apparently a rumor that the beloved disciple would not die before Jesus' second coming occurred. But he seems in fact to have died, perhaps recently. Thus the rumor is corrected by appealing to the literal meaning of Jesus' saying, "If it is my will that he remain until I come, what is that to you?" (21:22, 23). In 21:24–25 the Evangelist refers to "the disciple" (presumably the beloved disciple) as having provided written testimony and says that "we know that his testimony is true," which suggests some gap of time between his testimony and the final written product. The notice in 21:25 that the Gospel is only a small selection of all that Jesus said and did repeats the point made in 20:30.

For Reflection and Discussion

Review the arrest and trial of Jesus in John 18. What do the words and actions of Jesus reveal about his true identity?

How might the scene at the foot of the cross (John 19:25–27) shape your understanding of the church?

How does John 20 trace the development of Easter faith? On what do you base your own Easter faith?

PART THREE

John's Context

8

The Problem of "the Jews" in John's Gospel

The problem is that John's Gospel says some nasty things about a group that it calls "the Jews." Some people today, when they hear such negative talk about "the Jews," may assume a direct relationship between "the Jews" of John's Gospel and their Jewish neighbors who attend the local synagogue. During some periods of history, John's Gospel has been a vehicle for anti-Judaism.

The Greek term *hoi Ioudaioi* can be translated as "the Jews" or "the Judeans." Some texts in John's Gospel refer to the Jews in positive ways. For example, John speaks positively of "the Jews" who believed in Jesus (8:31–32, 12:11) and who were sympathetic bystanders at his raising Lazarus from the dead (11:31, 33, 36, 45). Also positive is Jesus' declaration in the dialogue with the Samaritan woman that "salvation is from the Jews" (4:22). John writes neutrally about the "Jewish rites of purification" (2:6) and the "Judean countryside" (3:22).

For the most part, however, the expression "the Jews" appears in negative contexts in John's Gospel. The most common negative context is debate with Jesus. Whereas in the Synoptic tradition, Jesus' debating partners are the Pharisees or scribes, in John's Gospel they are usually called "the Jews." The Jews send priests and Levites to inquire about John the Baptist (1:19). Nicodemus, "a leader of the Jews" (3:1), questions Jesus. The Jews in 5:10 object to Jesus healing a lame man on the Sabbath—and so on. These debates are literary productions, not direct recordings. Jesus' interrogators, whether the Jews or his own disciples, are always misunderstanding him. Their misunderstandings in turn become the occasion for Jesus to go beyond their objections and to reveal more about himself and his mission of revealing the Father. But in the process these literary foils—in many cases the Jews—look foolish, obtuse, or even hostile.

Besides looking like fools or worse, the Jews in John's Gospel are said to have persecuted Jesus because he healed on the Sabbath (5:16) and to have sought to kill Jesus (7:1). The disciples warn Jesus against going into Judean territory because the Jews there were seeking to kill him (11:8). The motif of "fear of the Jews" runs through Jesus' public ministry (9:22), his passion and death (19:38), and his resurrection appearances (20:19). Before his final journey to Jerusalem, Jesus no longer goes about openly among the Jews (11:54). The Jews are Jesus' chief opponents in John's Gospel.

It is not surprising that when John tells the story of Jesus' passion and death in chapters 18–19, the Jews play a major role. Whereas the Synoptic Gospels refer to Jesus' Jewish opponents in the passion narrative as "the chief priests and elders," in John they are simply Jews. The officers of the Jews (18:12) seize Jesus as part of the high priest Caiaphas's ironic plan that one man should die for the people (11:50, 18:14). When the Jews protest to Pontius Pilate that it is not lawful for them to put Jesus to death (18:31), the Jews press Pilate to have Jesus executed "because he has claimed to be the Son of God" (19:7). When Pilate asks to release Jesus, the Jews cry out, "If you release this man, you are no friend of the emperor." They object to the charge placed on Jesus' cross, "the King of the Jews." Instead they prefer, "This man said, 'I am the King of the Jews'" (19:19–22).

The implication of John's passion narrative is that without the pressure applied by the Jews to Pilate, Jesus would not have been crucified. In fact, John gives the impression that the Jews actually executed Jesus: "Then he [Pilate] handed him over to them [the Jews] to be crucified" (19:16). Throughout John's Gospel, then, the Jews oppose Jesus in debate, seek to kill him by various means, and finally convince the Roman governor to execute him.

Background

Why was John so negative toward the Jews? This is puzzling especially since it is virtually certain that John himself was a Jew—as were Jesus and the other early disciples. It is unlikely that John was simply criticizing Judeans from a Galilean perspective. To answer the question, we need to reflect on some sociological, historical, and theological factors that may have contributed to John's negative portrayal of the Jews. These factors may help us understand better what has been a disturbing feature in John's Gospel.

Sociological Factors

The Evangelist whom we call John wrote his story of Jesus near or in Palestine after AD 70, probably in the late first century. A very important event in Jewish history took place in AD 70: the Roman capture and destruction of Jerusalem and its temple. The Jewish historian Josephus blamed it on fanatics and bandits among the Jewish people. Whatever the precise cause may have been, the result was that Jews no longer had political control over their land or access to their most sacred site and principle of religious unity—the temple. The challenge facing all Jews after AD 70 was to reconstruct Judaism without the temple and the land.

Jews faced this challenge in various ways. The apocalyptists represented by 4 Ezra and 2 Baruch (two non-canonical apocalypses) looked forward to the imminent intervention of God that would spell the end of "this age" and the beginning of "the age to come." The political rebels or insurgents went underground but nourished their hope of gaining power by military means. They finally had their chance in the Bar Kokhba Revolt in AD 132–135 and failed. The early rabbis under Rabban Yohanan ben Zakkai developed a form of Judaism that joined devotion to the Torah, elements of Pharisaism, and other pre-70 traditions. This group later developed into the rabbinic movement that produced the Mishnah, the Talmuds, the Midrashim, and other writings.

Non-Jewish observers of early Christians in the late first century would have continued to look upon them as a Jewish sect, even if all the members were not ethnically Jewish. Such observers would have assumed that early Christians like John were Jews concerned with reconstructing Judaism around their Jewish hero,

Jesus of Nazareth. On the other hand, Jewish observers of the same early Christians would have looked on John and his colleagues as rivals in the task of reconstructing Judaism after the destruction of the Jerusalem temple.

In other words, Judaism of the late first century was at a crossroads. It could take the apocalyptic, the nationalistic, the rabbinic, or the Christian route. From the perspective of later history, the rabbinic way won out among Jews, and the Christian way developed into a separate religion. The apocalyptic way revived from time to time, and the nationalistic way has emerged again in modern Zionism. But things were not so clear in the first century.

The composition of John's Gospel should be viewed against the background of the crisis facing all Jews at that time and the rival claims among them to carry on the tradition of Judaism. *The negative portrait of the Jews in John's Gospel is part of an intra-Jewish quarrel.* There may be a connection between the Jews in John's Gospel and the emerging rabbinic movement led by Rabban Yohanan ben Zakkai. The Evangelist's use of "the Jews" may even refer to the Judean roots of that rival movement.

As John's Gospel shows, this quarrel became bitter. John intended his story of Jesus to be read on two levels: the time of Jesus' public activity (about AD 30), and the time of the intra-Jewish quarrel between his community and the Jews during the late first century. The Evangelist sought to identify the Jewish opponents of Jesus with the Jewish opponents of the Johannine community. And so just as the Jews in AD 30 misunderstand, persecute, and finally have Jesus killed, so the Jews in John's time are misunderstanding, persecuting, and perhaps even about to kill Christians.

The application of the term *aposynagogos* ("out of the syna-gogue") to the Christians in John's Gospel (9:22, 12:42, 16:2) may reflect the point to which the quarrel had come. The parallel in Matthew's Gospel is the description of the opponents ("scribes and Pharisees") as having control over "their synagogues" or "the synagogues of the hypocrites." Whether or not the so-called "blessing/cursing of the sectarians" that was added to the Jewish daily prayer had been enacted to force Christian Jews either to curse themselves or to leave the synagogue, some event or institu-tional policy was forcing a dramatic split between Christian Jews and other Jews in the late first century.

Quarrels within a religious movement are often bitter. In our own day, Jews argue about who is a Jew; Catholics debate about the proper interpretation and implementation of Vatican II; and liberal and conservative Protestants repeat the "battle for the Bible." In these quarrels, harsh and intemperate statements are made. The result is often division or a temporary truce. Such modern analogies can at least help us to appreciate the context in which John talked about the Jews. A Jew himself, he wrote in a highly emotional setting in which the future of Judaism was at stake. John was convinced that the Christian way was correct and that the other ways were not.

Political Factors

Besides the sociological factors, there may also have been a politi-cal factor in John's negative portrayal of the Jews. After the fall of Masada in AD 73/74, the Jews were a defeated people and under direct Roman control more thoroughly than ever before. At the same time, Jewish Christians had to explain an embarrassing fact about their hero, Jesus of Nazareth. He had been executed according to the Roman punishment of crucifixion reserved primarily for revolutionaries and slaves. The charge against him ("King of the Jews") suggests that the Roman governor considered him just another messianic pretender, a political rebel, a nationalist insurgent.

In the late first century, when Jews had no political power or influence, John and the other Evangelists to various extents shifted the responsibility for Jesus' death from the Romans to the Jews. The precise historical level of Jewish involvement in Jesus' passion and death is disputed among both Jewish and Christian scholars. Still there is little doubt that the Evangelists gradually made the Jewish leaders or the Jews in general into the prime movers and Pilate and the Romans into somewhat unwilling accomplices.

Josephus makes a similar move when he explains the destruction of Jerusalem in AD 70 as the inevitable result of Jewish fanatics having gained power and forcing the Romans to intervene. By blaming the Jews for Jesus' death, John explained away the embarrassing circumstances of Jesus' death and connected the Jews of Jesus' day with the rivals of his own community. This political apologetic on John's part, ingenious in the situation perhaps, has had unfortunate long-term consequences for Christian-Jewish relations in the centuries since.

Theological Factors

In John's portrait of Jesus and the Jews, he assumes a dualistic theological framework. For many years, John's Gospel had been read as the most "Greek" Gospel. That changed with the discovery of the Dead Sea scrolls in 1947, in which eagerness for knowledge and the sharp contrast between light and darkness appear as major themes. While acknowledging the ultimate power of God, the Qumran people (probably Essenes) divided all present reality into two camps. The children of light do the deeds of light under the leadership of the Angel of Light, and the children of darkness do the deeds of darkness under the leadership of the Prince of Darkness. At the divine visitation (the Last Judgment and the full coming of God's kingdom), God will vindicate and reward the righteous, and punish and destroy wickedness forever. This Jewish form of modified dualism found its way into early Christianity and received its strongest expressions in Paul's letters and John's Gospel. So it is not surprising that John placed his rivals who are designated as "the Jews" alongside "the world" with the children of darkness. In such dualistic thinking, matters are black and white, and "the Jews" end up on the wrong side of the dividing line.

Also, John locates Jesus and the Jews with reference to various Jewish institutions and traditions. John responded to the crisis posed by the events of AD 70 by showing how various Jewish titles and figures—Wisdom, Word, Lamb of God, Messiah, Son of God, King of Israel, and Son of Man—apply to Jesus. He also showed how Jesus gave new meaning to the celebrations of Jewish festivals such as the Sabbath, Passover, Tabernacles, and Hanukkah. Whereas the Torah was given through Moses, the premise and goal of the Torah ("grace and truth") for John came through the Word made flesh, Jesus (1:17). Jesus was the one about whom Moses and the prophets wrote (1:45). Although John portrayed Jesus as an observant Jew who regularly made pilgrimages to Jerusalem for the holy days, John (like other early Christians) was more interested in how the Torah stood with reference to Jesus and how the Scriptures pointed toward him than in how exactly Jesus observed the Torah.

Dealing with the Problem

The problem of the portrayal of the Jews in John's Gospel is basically a Christian problem, though it surely has had implications for Jews. The responsibility for dealing with it resides primarily with those who affirm that John's Gospel is part of Christian Scripture and is authentic testimony to Christ. Two avenues open to those who want to do something about the problem are educating people to recognize the shape of the problem, and reflecting on what and how our biblical translations communicate.

Educating people means recognizing the shape of the problem.

This involves awareness of the historical circumstances in which John's Gospel was composed. John was a Jewish Christian. He wrote for a largely Jewish Christian audience living in tension with other Jews in the late first century. He was trying to show that the Christian movement was the authentic response to the crisis posed by the destruction of the Jerusalem temple. His negative comments about the Jews had a specific setting. They were not intended to be what we call anti-Semitic because they came from within Judaism, and attempts to label John's Gospel as intrinsically anti-Semitic or anti-Jewish are anachronistic and unfair.

Nevertheless, Christians must be willing also to admit the anti-Jewish or anti-Semitic potential of John's representation of the Jews. When taken out of the late first century setting within Judaism, the Gospel can be read as anti-Jewish, and that has been done. This is where the liberating function of historical study comes in. What was perhaps understandable in a first-century, intra-Jewish context need not be repeated for all time or raised to the status of abstract truth. Those who know history are not doomed to repeat it. John's treatment of the Jews is a powerful argument for the need for Christians (and Jews) to become more sensitive to the historical origins of our Scriptures.

Another part of the problem involves biblical translations.

With each Good Friday, I grow more uncomfortable about what parishioners may understand about the words and actions of "the Jews" in the reading of John's story of Jesus' suffering and death. What images do they get of Jews? Do they make connections between them and their Jewish neighbors and coworkers? Does John's Gospel add to their negative stereotypes about Jews? Some biblical scholars and church leaders suggest that in our translations "the Jews" needs to be modified to read "some Jews" or "the Jewish leaders" or even "the Judeans" to break the pattern of blaming the Jews collectively for Jesus' death.

Although many (including me) hesitate to tamper with the Gospel text, there are precedents for doing such things. In antiquity the Jewish targumists produced Aramaic paraphrases of the Hebrew Bible in order to make sure that the theological content of the biblical text was correctly understood. Today some Bible translators adopt what is called the *dynamic equivalence* theory of translation. According to this theory, the translator must first understand the original text as precisely as possible and then attempt to say in the language of the translation what the original author was trying to communicate. Since the *thought* is the most important concern, there is no need to reflect formally (or woodenly) the word order and vocabulary of the original text.

From the perspective of history, "some Jews" or "the Jewish leaders" are accurate translations. But they do not really capture John's dualism or his fondness for collective nouns, and thus may distort John's text. "Judeans" does break the connections between ancient Jews and modern Jews, but it is primarily a geographical term and fails to convey the religious aspect of the Greek expression *hoi Ioudaioi* ("the Jews"). So putting what we know about "the Jews" in John's Gospel into a translation remains a challenge.

I hesitate to turn a Good Friday homily into a lecture on the evils of anti-Semitism. Yet the problem posed by the Johannine portrait of the Jews should at least be woven into Christian preaching and teaching at various points in the lectionary cycle. Above all, our people must be instructed about the intra-Jewish debate in which John's Gospel took shape. On a more general level, they may also need help in grasping some points of Christian theology that have been clarified through Vatican II's document *Nostra Aetate* 4 and recent Christian-Jewish dialogue: that the claim that Jesus "fulfilled" the Jewish Scriptures does not mean that he emptied them of meaning; that the charge of deicide against Jews is a theological absurdity; and that God's choosing of and gifts to Israel are irrevocable. Also, we need to see that Jesus lived and died as a Jew, that the first generation of Christians were Jews, and that their willingness to incorporate non-Jews into the people of God was based on the Jewishness of Jesus himself. (In this chapter I have drawn on material from my essay on "'The Jews' in John's Gospel," *The Bible Today* 27 [1989] 203–209.)

PART FOUR

John's Gospel in
Christian Life

9

John's Gospel in the Church's Lectionary

A lectionary is a book containing the Scripture readings assigned for the Sundays, major feast days, and weekdays in the church's year that are to be used in connection with its celebrations of the Eucharist. In response to the directives of the Second Vatican Council, there was developed in the late 1960s a three-year cycle for Sundays (A, B, C) and a two-year cycle for weekdays (I, II).

In the three-year Sunday cycle, most of the Gospel readings come from Matthew (Year A), Mark (Year B), and Luke (Year C), respectively. The Old Testament readings are generally chosen with an eye toward a connection to the Gospel text. The responsorial psalm provides a bridge between the Old Testament and Gospel readings. The epistle (second) readings are on a separate cycle, through there are often thematic links to the other readings.

For weekdays during Ordinary Time, there are continuous readings from Mark, Matthew, and Luke, respectively, each year. There are also readings from the Old Testament books and the New Testament epistles arranged in two cycles (Year I is odd-numbered years, and Year II is even-numbered years), with the responsorial psalms serving as bridge texts. The weekday readings for the Advent, Lenten, and Easter seasons remain the same every year.

Where does John's Gospel fit into the church's lectionary? We might say that John fills the gaps. Or better, we might say that John provides spiritual depth at the most important points during the liturgical year. Thus John can be called the Evangelist for all seasons. The Appendix on pages 133–136 provides a full list of the passages from John's Gospel that appear in the current lectionary. A glance at that list will show that John's Gospel is most prominent in the seasons of Lent and Easter, and that almost all of John's Gospel appears over the course of the three-year Sunday and two-year daily lectionary cycles. Nevertheless, the absence of a Year of John over one separate year can make it seem that John's Gospel is somewhat neglected.

On many Sundays in the Lenten and Easter seasons, the Gospel passage is taken from John, and on Good Friday every year John's passion narrative (chapters 18—19) is read in full. Also, in the Year B (Mark), selections from John 6 (the Bread of Life discourse) are spread over five Sundays in late summer.

In what follows I will discuss briefly the place of John's Gospel in the church's lectionary for the Sundays in Lent, Easter, and Ordinary Time, respectively. I will also provide a sample exposition for a set of readings for one of the Sundays in each of those three seasons. These expositions are adaptations of my essays that originally appeared in "The Word" column in *America* magazine.

John's Gospel during Lent

In Year A, the Gospel readings for the Third, Fourth, and Fifth Sundays of Lent are three very long and beautiful passages from John's Gospel:

- Jesus' encounter with the Samaritan woman (4:5–42)
- Jesus' healing of the man born blind (9:1–41)
- Jesus' restoring Lazarus to life (11:1–45).

These same texts may be used in Years B and C, in connection with the Rite of Christian Initiation for Adults. They feature lively narratives and dialogues, and in various ways describe how religious seekers gradually come to believe in Jesus.

In Year B for the Third, Fourth, and Fifth Sundays of Lent, the selections from John's Gospel are about

- Jesus identifying his own body as the temple (2:13–25)
- Jesus as the Son of Man whose death can give eternal life (3:14–21)
- Jesus foretelling his death and Resurrection as the "hour" of his glory (12:20–33).

In Year C, the story of the woman taken in adultery (8:1–11) fits well in the sequence of texts from Luke's Gospel that emphasize God's mercy toward sinners.

On the weekdays during Lent in both Years I and II, readings from the Book of Signs (chapters 4—5 and 7—12) and from the beginning of the Book of Glory (chapter 13) provide the Gospel texts for the second half of the season.

To illustrate the use of John's Gospel during Lent, I will focus on Jesus' encounter with the Samaritan woman (4:5–42), which is read on the third Sunday of Lent in Year A (and may also be read in Years B and C). It is paired with passages from Exodus 17:3–7; Psalm 95:1–2, 6–9; and Romans 5:1–2, 6–8. These readings contribute in various ways to the theme of satisfying spiritual thirst, a concept that is especially appropriate for Lent and in particular for those preparing to receive the sacraments of Christian initiation.

Example 1: Living Water
Third Sunday of Lent (A)
Readings: Exodus 17:3–7; Psalm 95:1–2, 6–9; Romans 5:1–2, 5–8; John 4:5–42

> Where do you get that living water?
>
> —John 4:11

On the literal level, "living water" is the opposite of stagnant water. It is water that flows from a spring or river, and so it is fresh and pure. On the spiritual level, living water is what we ultimately hope for—right relationship with God and eternal life. The Scripture readings for the Third Sunday of Lent revolve around the different senses of living water and how our thirst for God may be satisfied.

Today's reading from Exodus 17 concerns the wilderness generation's thirst for fresh drinking water and wholesome food. Having escaped from slavery in Egypt, the people grumble against Moses and his failure to supply them with food and drink. They murmur against Moses and indirectly against God, when they ask, "Why did you ever make us leave Egypt? Was it just to have us die here of thirst?" Their rebellion at Massah and Meribah (these place names mean "testing" and "rebellion," respectively) becomes in Psalm 95 the example of ancient Israel's failure to trust in God's loving care. Eventually through God's miraculous intervention, Moses supplies living water for the people in the wilderness.

The long narrative about the encounter between Jesus and the Samaritan woman from John 4 also concerns thirst and living water. It takes place at the well near Shechem, the Samaritans' traditional place of worship. Here the water is what Jesus reveals about himself and his heavenly Father. From Jesus' request for a drink of water, the conversation moves in the direction of the living water, spiritual worship, and true food that Jesus alone can provide.

This story has an intricate structure. First Jesus converses with the Samaritan woman. Next he promises living water. Then the woman identifies him as a prophet. The center of the account is Jesus' affirmation that salvation is from the Jews (his people) and that soon God will be worshipped "in Spirit and truth." Then the story goes into reverse. The woman identifies Jesus as the Messiah. Next Jesus promises true food. Finally

Jesus converses with Samaritans. This kind of structure is called "concentric," and it appears frequently in the Bible and in other ancient writings.

Here Jesus deals openly and compassionately with Samaritans, persons regarded by Judeans and Galileans as at best marginally Jewish. And a Samaritan woman with a dubious past becomes the person through whom Jesus' message is conveyed to other Samaritans. In John's Gospel she in effect functions as the first Christian missionary when she tells others about Jesus.

The story in John also bears witness to a dramatic progression in faith regarding Jesus. The woman first identifies Jesus as a Judean, like many others in their time. Next when Jesus correctly tells the woman about her past, she identifies him as a prophet. Then the woman begins to suspect that he might be the Messiah. Finally after other Samaritans converse with Jesus for two days, they declare that he is "the savior of the world."

At the center of the story, Jesus promises a new kind of worship "in Spirit and truth." Early in the story he promised to give "living water," and later on he speaks about "my food." Christian readers will naturally make connections with baptism and the Eucharist. This worship "in Spirit and truth" is rooted in and faithful to ancient Israel's traditions, is inextricably connected with the person of Jesus, and is open to all kinds of persons.

Paul's reflection on Christian hope in Romans 5 can help us understand better the dynamic of spiritual thirst. It shows how faith, hope and love work together and form the framework of Christian life. Hope begins with God's love for us. Paul points to Christ's death for us sinners as proof of God's love for us. God continues to pour his love into our hearts through the Holy Spirit, and we need to respond to that gift with love for God and others. The way we participate in the paschal mystery is through faith. Through faith we have peace with God and ourselves, and we have access to God's grace. Our Christian life receives its forward motion from hope and is sustained by hope for eternal life. Our greatest hope is the glory of God, and this hope does not disappoint us. Another way to describe Paul's point is to say that our life consists in seeking and finding "living water" and "true food" in and through Christ.

Praying with Scripture

Imagine yourself as a thirsty and hungry Israelite in the wilderness. What do you want from Moses and God?

What makes possible the progression in faith regarding Jesus in John 4? What role does the Samaritan woman play?

How does your own experience of thirst help you understand Paul's dynamic of faith, hope, and love?

John's Gospel during Easter

John's Gospel was written from the perspective of the "hour" of Jesus. Both the Evangelist and his community were convinced that Jesus had really died, been raised from the dead, returned to his heavenly Father, and now reigns in glory.

In the Sacred Triduum of Holy Week each year, there are readings from John's Gospel:

- Jesus washing the feet of his disciples on Holy Thursday (13:1–15)
- the entire passion narrative for Good Friday (18:1–19:42)
- the empty-tomb account for Easter Day (20:1–9).

On the second Sunday of Easter, the Gospel readings from John for Years A, B, and C concern the appearances of the risen Jesus to his disciples (minus Thomas) first on Easter afternoon and then to the full complement of disciples (including Thomas) on the following Sunday (20:19–31). On the Third Sunday in Year C, the Gospel text (21:1–19) describes the appearance to the disciples while fishing in the Sea of Galilee.

Each of the three Sunday cycles in Easter features parts of the Good Shepherd discourse (10:1–10, 10:11–18, 10:27–30) and the High Priestly prayer (17:1–10, 17:11–19, 17:20–27). Interspersed among the passages for the other Sundays in the Easter season are various selections from Jesus' farewell discourses in John 13–17. They concern love (13:31–35), keeping Jesus' memory alive (14:1–12), the love commandment and the Holy Spirit (14:15–21), the Paraclete (14:23–29), and the vine and the branches (15:1–8, 15:9–17).

To illustrate how John's Gospel fits in the Easter season, I will focus on the allegory of the vine and the branches in John 15 and develop the theme of Christian mysticism. On the Fifth Sunday of Easter in Year B, that passage is paired with Paul's testimony about his experience of the risen Christ in Acts 9:26–31 and the exhortation in 1 John 3:18–21 about doing the truth.

Example 2: Christian Mysticism

Fifth Sunday of Easter (B)

Readings: Acts 9:26–31; Psalm 22:26–28, 30–32; 1 John 3:18–24; John 15:1–8

> I am the true vine, and my Father is the vine grower
> —John 15:1

At its most basic level, the word "mysticism" refers to a direct, intimate union of a person with God through contemplation and love. The Scripture readings for the Fifth Sunday of Easter can help explain why every serious Christian can and should be a mystic.

The allegory of the vine in John 15 teaches that believers in Jesus are related to him in a vital and organic way, and that their discipleship entails abiding in that relationship and demands faithfulness to it. An allegory is a literary device by which each element in a story is equated with someone or something else. Here the vine is Jesus, the farmer/vine grower is God the Father, and the branches are those who follow Jesus. Today's text is part of Jesus' farewell discourse in John 14—17, whose setting is Jesus' Last Supper with his disciples. The main topic is how the community formed by the earthly Jesus can carry on when he is no longer bodily or physically present as he was during his earthly ministry. The point is that the life-giving Spirit of Jesus will still be present and active among his disciples and their successors.

In the vine allegory, Jesus is the vine in the sense that his vital energy courses through the whole plant and its branches and serves as its source of life and dynamism. The Father is the farmer or vine grower who tends to the vine at every stage in its existence. The disciples are the branches who depend on both the vine and the vine grower for their growth and continuing care.

The vine grower's activities include cutting away the dead branches and pruning back the live branches so that they may produce fruit ever more abundantly. They live and bear fruit or shrivel and die, depending on whether they keep Jesus' commandments to believe and love. The disciples whom Jesus addresses have already been "pruned" through his word—that is, they have been cleansed from what prevents their bearing fruit. But just as branches cannot bear fruit unless they remain connected to the vine, so disciples of Jesus cannot bear fruit unless they remain or abide in Jesus. Those who fail to abide in Jesus can expect to be cut off, withered up, and burned as fuel for the fire. The allegory of the vine is basic for understanding Christian mysticism. The defining character of Christian mysticism is direct, intimate union with God through the person of Jesus.

Today's reading from 1 John 3 develops the concept of Christian mysticism from the perspective of the response expected from disciples of Jesus. First, they must express their relationship with God through Jesus "in deed and truth." That expression evokes the Johannine concept of doing the truth. In the context of John's Gospel, the truth is not merely something to be contemplated, talked about, and admired. Rather, the truth is something to be done, acted upon, and expressed concretely. For

John, the truth is incarnate in Jesus as the Way, the Truth and the Life.

Doing the truth is best expressed by keeping the two great commandments found in John's Gospel: "believe in the name of his Son, Jesus Christ, and love one another just as he commanded us." Those who keep these commandments will "remain in him and he in them." Thus Christian mysticism demands a response from the believer in the practical arena of everyday life. Doing the truth involves believing and loving, all in the framework of abiding in Christ.

The prime biblical example of the Christian mystic is the apostle Paul. The story of Paul's conversion and call to become the apostle to the Gentiles is told three times in Acts, in chapters 9, 22, and 26, respectively. Today's reading from Acts 9 describes the aftermath of his transformation from being the enemy of the early Christian movement to becoming the instrument chosen by God to bring the gospel to non-Jews.

On his own testimony (see Philippians 3:4–11), Paul's experience of the risen Jesus on the road to Damascus was so powerful that it made his past accomplishments in the practice of Pharisaic Judaism seem like so much rubbish. From then on, Paul's whole life and energy were consumed in sharing that experience and its consequences by showing others their new dignity in Christ and encouraging them to act in ways appropriate to their new status in Christ. The classic expression of Christian mysticism comes from Paul himself: "I live, not longer I, but Christ lives in me" (Galatians 2:20).

Christian mysticism is not limited to a tiny minority of religious professionals or spiritual virtuosi. Rather, Christian mysticism, as expressed in John's Gospel and Paul's writings, is available to all who believe, love, and abide in Jesus and his Father.

Praying With Scripture

How does the allegory of the vine help you understand better Christian life in general and Christian mysticism in particular?

What is "truth" for you? Does the Gospel of John's concept of doing the truth add to your appreciation of truth?

In what sense is Paul a prototype of the Christian mystic? What does this mean for your understanding of mysticism?

John's Gospel in Ordinary Time

On the Second Sunday in Ordinary Time in each of the three cycles, there is a reading from an early part of John's Gospel: John the Baptist's testimony about Jesus as the Lamb of God (1:29–34 in Year A), Jesus' call of his first disciples (1:35–42 in Year B), and the wedding feast at Cana (2:1–12 in Year C). But the most extensive material from John's Gospel appears as a series of five passages from Jesus' Bread of Life discourse in John 6. These texts interrupt the sequence of selections from Mark's Gospel from the Seventeenth to the Twenty-First Sundays in Year B. In the late summer these passages provide a wonderful opportunity to reflect on Jesus as the Wisdom of God and to consider the mystery of the Eucharist in the context of Johannine theology.

Example 3: Wisdom's Banquet

Twentieth Sunday in Ordinary Time (B)

Readings: Proverbs 9:1–6; Psalm 34:2–7; Ephesians 5:15–20; John 6:51–58

> Unless you eat the flesh of the Son of Man and drink
> his blood, you have no life in you.
>
> —John 6:53

During the series of reflections on Jesus' bread of life discourse in John 6, we see repeatedly how the Old Testament passages chosen for each Sunday cast fresh light on Jesus and the Eucharist. Today's selection from Proverbs 9 reminds us that the Eucharist is also Wisdom's banquet.

In Proverbs and other Wisdom writings, it is customary to represent Wisdom as a female figure. She is frequently contrasted with Lady Folly. One of the motifs associated with Lady Wisdom is her banquet. In antiquity a banquet was an occasion to share wisdom, with food and drink for both body and soul. The practice survives in our word *symposium*, which means literally "drinking together."

According to Proverbs 9, Wisdom builds a sturdy house and prepares a sumptuous feast of meat, wine, and other choice foods. Having readied her feast, she sends out her maids to issue an invitation to come to her house. The invitation is worded in such a way that there is no doubt that those who accept it will gain the spiritual and practical insight to advance in the way of understanding.

In their hymns and creeds, early Christians often identified Jesus as the Wisdom of God. The bread of life discourse indicates that the Christian community shaped by John's teaching regarded the Eucharist as Wisdom's banquet where they shared in the divine wisdom personified by Jesus. They viewed the Eucharist as holding out the possibility of greater friendship with God and a deeper personal relationship with the one whom they confessed to be the bread of life.

As Jesus draws near the end of his discourse in John 6, his language becomes stronger and more shockingly eucharistic. He talks about eating the flesh of the Son of Man and drinking his blood. He speaks about feeding on his flesh, and identifies his flesh as real food and his blood as real drink. The wording is graphic and even offensive, especially to Jews. It is intended to make explicit the connection between the eucharistic elements and the person of Jesus. John 6 more than makes up for the absence of a meal narrative in John 13—17. In this context the Eucharist is more than an analogy, metaphor, or symbol. It is a realistic sharing in Jesus the Wisdom of God, and it promises a share in God's own life and therefore in eternal life.

Today's reading from Ephesians 5 reminds us that the wisdom we have through Jesus must become real in our everyday lives. It warns that the present time is difficult and challenging, and so demands our caution and practical wisdom. What gives shape and direction to Christian life is the continuing effort to discern the will of God. Instead of giving in to drunkenness and debauchery, Paul recommends being filled with the Holy Spirit and singing hymns to God. And he identifies the basic task of

Christian life as "giving thanks to God the Father at all times and for everything in the name of our Lord Jesus Christ." Giving thanks, of course, is exactly what the word *Eucharist* means.

Praying With Scripture

Does the idea of the Eucharist as Wisdom's banquet enrich your understanding of the Eucharist? How and why?

What effect does the realistic language used in today's selection from John 6 have on you? Does it shock you?

How do you make connections between the Eucharist and your everyday life?

10

John's Gospel and the Spiritual Exercises

The Spiritual Exercises developed by Ignatius of Loyola are profoundly biblical. Indeed, they represent a way of assimilating and actualizing the biblical vision. Not only do the four Gospels provide most of the content for the meditations, but also the most pivotal exercises have deep biblical roots.

This chapter points out some important similarities between John's Gospel and eight pivotal moments in the Spiritual Exercises.

Seeking and Finding God's Will

The stated goal of the Spiritual Exercises is to rid oneself of all "disordered tendencies" and "to seek and find the divine will as to the management of one's life for the salvation of the soul." Experienced spiritual directors often ask retreatants to articulate at least in a preliminary fashion what they seek and desire most from the retreat.

John's Gospel has a similar purpose, and so it can be a biblical help toward achieving that goal. In his encounter with his first prospective disciples in John 1:35–42, Jesus' first words are, "What are you looking for?" When the two men find it difficult to formulate an answer, Jesus invites them to "come and see." It is essential that those making the Spiritual Exercises try to express at the outset what they are seeking, to keep asking that question throughout the retreat, and to let their encounter with Jesus through Scripture and prayer refine and even transform their answers.

Near the end of John's Gospel, the risen Jesus puts a similar question to Mary Magdalene as she tries to understand who the mysterious stranger at Jesus' tomb might be (20:15). Jesus asks her, "For whom are you looking?" Only when Jesus calls Mary by name does she recognize that the stranger is the risen Jesus and that she is ready to fulfill her role as the apostle to the apostles. In her encounter with the risen Jesus, Mary has found the one whom she was seeking. The basic aim of John's Gospel and the Spiritual Exercises from beginning to end is the same: to help those who seek God's will to find it through a personal relationship with the risen Jesus.

The Principle and Foundation

The aim of the First Week of the Spiritual Exercises is to look at ourselves and the world around us, and try to see what disordered tendencies may be getting in the way of our spiritual freedom. The starting point is the meditation known as "the Principle and Foundation." Using language that often sounds more philosophical than theological, the text defines the purpose of human existence as "to praise, reverence, and serve God the Lord" and in this way to save one's soul. It goes on to explain that we ought to use all created things in the service of reaching that goal and to avoid whatever may hinder us from doing so. And so it promotes a kind of spiritual "indifference" aimed primarily at finding what is most conducive toward achieving the end for which we have been created.

But why should we want to praise, reverence, and serve God the Lord? The Christ-centered vision of creation provided by the prologue to John's Gospel (1:1–18) can help us answer that question. There Jesus is identified as the Word or Wisdom of God, who participated in the work of creation and remains the light that shines in the darkness. He is the revealer and the revelation of God, and through him we can become children of God and so stand alongside Jesus as the Son of God. By becoming "flesh" (human) and making his dwelling among us, Jesus as the Word of God makes available "grace and truth" to us all, and as "God the only Son" he serves as the interpreter or exegete of his heavenly Father.

The Call of Christ the King

After several meditations on sin and its consequences on both the general and personal levels, the Second Week of the Spiritual Exercises begins with the call of Christ the King. Ignatius first asks us to consider an attractive human king, his call to join him in conquering the world, and the response that good subjects ought to give. The imagery, of course, reflects Ignatius's own background as a soldier and a courtier, and his historical context in the late Middle Ages and the defense of Spain and many other parts of Europe against the inroads of Islam. Then Ignatius asks that we imagine this king to be "Christ our Lord, King eternal," and that his call to his subjects is "to conquer all the world and all enemies and so to enter into the glory of my Father." The proper response would be for his subjects to offer themselves fully to the service of such a king.

With its overture of titles applied to Jesus in chapter 1, John's Gospel can help us appreciate better the greatness of Christ the King as he issues the call to follow him and become part of his great undertaking. He is no ordinary leader or king. Rather, he is the Word of God, the Son of God, the Messiah, the Prophet, the Lamb of God, the Teacher, the King of Israel, and the glorious Son of Man. His project is to draw all persons and indeed all creation closer to his heavenly Father. The enthusiasm that he creates among his first followers is clear from their responses to his invitation ("come and see") to be with him and share in his mission. However, as the elaborate trial scene before Pilate in 18:28—19:16 shows, his kingship is not of this world and involves suffering and death.

Trinity and Incarnation

Closely connected with the call of Christ the King is the meditation on the Incarnation—that is, how and why the Word of God (Jesus) "became flesh." The obvious starting point for the divine side of this mystery is John 1:14. Ignatius tries to catch the human side by directing us to Luke's infancy narrative and the pivotal role of Mary in accepting her call to be the mother of the Messiah. But he also presents the Incarnation as the result of a decision made jointly by the Three Persons of the Holy Trinity. He invites us to imagine the Three Persons looking down from heaven on the sorry state of humankind on earth and deciding, "Let us work the redemption of the human race." This is to be carried out through the Incarnation of Jesus the Son of God.

The Trinitarian perspective of Ignatius's theology is at its core in harmony with the Gospel of John. The prologue to John's Gospel introduces Jesus as the Word of God and the Son of God, two titles that were very influential in arriving at the statements of later church councils about the Trinity. In becoming one of us, the Son of God provided us with the perfect mediator with his Father. And the Son's principal role is to reveal his Father to us. The accusation raised by the Jews against Jesus that he was "making himself equal to God" (5:18) was in John's view perfectly correct. John's Gospel reaches its climax when Thomas confesses the risen Jesus to be "my Lord and my God" (20:28). And in his farewell discourse in chapters 14—16, Jesus makes frequent mention of the Holy Spirit/Paraclete, who will continue the work of God in the world when Jesus is no longer physically present on earth.

Contemplating Gospel Scenes

Most of the meditations for the Second to the Fourth Week of the Exercises take their starting point from scenes in the Gospels. Ignatius moves from Gospel to Gospel. But many directors today suggest staying with one Gospel for most of the contemplations, so that there may be more unity and coherence in theological perspective. An excellent guide for those who want to work with John's Gospel is David M. Stanley's *I Encountered God! The Spiritual Exercises with the Gospel of Saint John*. A Canadian Jesuit, Stanley (1914–96) was one of the most influential figures in bringing the fresh insights of European (especially French) biblical scholarship to North America in the 1960s and 1970s. He was also a distinguished New Testament scholar in his own right, an expert in the Spiritual Exercises, and a very popular and effective retreat director.

The most distinctive contribution in how Ignatius approaches Gospel scenes comes in the application of the senses: sight, hearing, taste, touch, and smell. Ignatius encourages retreatants to use their imaginations and make themselves observers at or even participants in the events described by the Evangelists. For example, take the anointing of Jesus by Mary of Bethany in John 12:1–8. In Ignatian contemplation we are encouraged to imagine ourselves as guests at the meal in Lazarus's house. See the room in which the meal is held. Touch the bread that is served. Taste the food. Look around at the various characters: Lazarus, Martha, Mary, Judas, and Jesus. See what Mary does in anointing Jesus' feet and drying them with her hair. Observe the shock on the part of the other guests. Listen to what Judas says about the waste, and to Jesus' defense of Mary's actions. And smell the expensive perfume, thus appreciating the Evangelist's comment that "the house was filled with fragrance of the perfume." For a full treatment of methods of Ignatian contemplation applied to Gospel texts, see my *Meeting St. Luke Today*, pp. 112–118.

The Two Standards

Early in the Second Week, Ignatius places before us two leaders—Christ and Satan—and urges us to make explicit which of the two we intend to follow. Satan presides in Babylon, in a smoky and horrible place. He enlists the services of demons. He traps people by riches, honor, and pride, and so leads them further into other vices. By contrast, Christ presides in Jerusalem, in a beautiful and attractive place. He enlists all kinds of persons to spread his teachings and leads them into a life of virtue through poverty, contempt for worldly honors, and humility. The challenge is to decide under whose banner or standard you will choose to serve. While the choice may seem easy, carrying through on it during one's lifetime may not be so easy.

Ignatius's imagery and thought are rooted in the dualistic thinking found in Second Temple Judaism and in the writings of Paul and John. This kind of thought is expressed most clearly in one of the Dead Sea (Qumran) scrolls known as the *Rule of the Community*. God remains sovereign over all creation. But God has temporarily entrusted the governance of the world to two powers, the Angel of Light and the Prince of Darkness. Those who follow the Angel of Light are the children of light and do the deeds of light. Those who follow the Prince of Darkness are the children of darkness and do the deeds of darkness. This dualism will come to an end in the divine visitation or judgment. Then the children of light will be vindicated and rewarded, and the children of darkness will be condemned, punished, and annihilated.

This kind of dualistic thinking underlies the theology in John's Gospel to a large extent. Jesus is the equivalent of the

Angel of Light, and Satan is the Prince of Darkness. The followers of Jesus are now children of God and do the deeds of light, whereas their opponents (the world, the Jews) follow Satan and do the deeds of darkness. At the Last Judgment, the former will be vindicated and the latter will be punished.

The major difference from the Qumran version of this dualism is the Johannine (and Pauline) conviction that the divine visitation has already begun through the Incarnation of Jesus the Son of God and the "hour" that embraces his passion, death, Resurrection, and exaltation. For believers in Jesus, eternal life has already begun, and the challenge they face in the present is to do what is appropriate to their identity as children of God. The two great commandments now are to believe in Jesus as the revealer and the revelation of God, and to love God and one another.

Making a Decision

Near the end of the Second Week, Ignatius prepares retreatants to make a decision (also called an election). The decision may involve choosing a state of life (marriage, religious life) or a profession (business, medicine). Or it may simply be a matter of reaffirming commitments already made, making resolutions about lifestyle, or correcting bad habits.

The ultimate decision, of course, is that of the Two Standards—choosing to serve God under the banner of Christ. One of the primary purposes of John's Gospel is to help the reader come to a decision about Jesus. And one of the Evangelist's key words is *krisis*, that is, a judgment or decision. Belief in Jesus becomes the criterion by which all are to be judged (see 3:17–21). Indeed, the stated purpose of the whole Gospel is that those who read it may come to believe in Jesus as the Messiah and Son of God (20:31).

John encourages practical action on the part of Jesus' disciples. In return for the gifts that God has given them through Christ, they are challenged with a wide array of verbs: to come, follow, see, know, believe, abide, testify, and love. Like Ignatius, John is a practical theologian who expects Christians to take initiative, discern, and find what they seek. The Johannine ideal of Christian life is best captured by the phrase "doing the truth." Truth is something to be acted on, not simply to be talked about or admired.

Contemplation to Obtain Love

Having brought retreatants to making a decision for Jesus, Ignatius makes them face the reality of Jesus' passion and death in the Third Week and enter into the joy of Jesus' Resurrection in the Fourth Week. The various scenes in John 18—21 can provide ample material for both mind and imagination in these exercises. The Spiritual Exercises end in climactic fashion with a meditation on love.

By way of introduction, Ignatius insists that love should manifest itself in deeds (a strong emphasis in the Gospel of John), and that love consists in a sharing of goods. He then bids us to reflect on four aspects of God's love: God's gifts to me, God's gift of himself to me, God's labors for me, and God as giver and gift. Genuine love starts with a recognition and appreciation of God's love for us.

Love is a major theme throughout John's Gospel, but especially in the farewell discourse in John 13—17. There are three dimensions in this Gospel's concept of love: God's love for us, our love for God, and our love for one another. The basic insight is that God has loved us first and has proven that love by sending his Son among us. Conscious that the Father loves him, Jesus in turn shows his love for his disciples and those who become disciples through them (John 17). In laying down his life for others, the Jesus of John's Gospel is the perfect exemplar of love. "For God so loved the world that he gave his only Son, so that everyone who believes in him may not perish but may have eternal life" (3:16). The proper response to God's love for us is the prayer that ends and summarizes the Spiritual Exercises:

"Take, Lord, and receive all my liberty, my memory, my understanding, and my entire will—all that I have and call my own. You have given it all to me. To you, Lord, I return it. Everything is yours; do with it what you will. Give me only your love and your grace. That is enough for me."

For Reflection and Discussion

Why have you chosen to follow Christ the King and stand under his standard? What difference does it make in your life?

Imagine yourself as a participant at the wedding in Cana (John 2:1–12). What do you see, hear, taste, touch, and smell?

Do you need to make an important decision? How might John's Gospel be of help?

Readings from John's Gospel in the Lectionary

In the Sunday lectionary used by the Roman Catholic and other Christian churches, there is a three-year cycle of Gospel readings that features a different Synoptic Gospel each year: Matthew (A), Mark (B), and Luke (C). Selections from John's Gospel are interspersed in each of the three cycles and on major liturgical feasts. For the weekdays there are two cycles in Ordinary Time (I and II) and one cycle in Advent, Lent, and Easter. John's Gospel is prominent in the second half of Lent and throughout most of the Easter season. The following lists show where texts from John's Gospel appear in the current lectionary.

A. John's Gospel by Liturgical Seasons

1. Sundays in Lent

Year A, 3rd to 5th: 4:5–42; 9:1–41; 11:1–45.

Year B, 3rd to 5th: 2:13–25; 3:14–21; 12:20–33.

Year C, 5th: 8:1–11.

2. Sundays in Easter

Year A, 2nd, 4th to 7th: 20:19–31; 10:1–10; 14:1–12; 14:15–21; 17:1–11.

Year B, 2nd, 4th to 7th: 20:19–31; 10:11–18; 15:1–8; 15:9–17; 17:11–19.

Year C, 2nd to 7th: 20:19–31; 21:1–19; 10:27–30; 13:31–33; 14:23–29; 17:20–26.

3. Sundays in Ordinary Time

Year A, 2nd: 1:29–34.

Year B, 2nd: 1:35–42; 17th to 21st: 6:1–15; 6:24–35;
6:41–51; 6:51–58; 6:60–69.

Year C, 2nd: 2:1–12.

4. Major Feasts

Years A, B, and C, Christmas Day: 1:1–18; Holy Thursday:
13:1–15; Good Friday: 18:1–19:42; Easter Day: 20:1–9;
Vigil of Pentecost: 7:37–39; Pentecost: 20:19–23.

5. Other Feasts

Year A, Trinity Sunday: 3:16–18; Corpus Christi: 6:51–58.

Year B, 3rd Sunday of Advent: 1:6–8, 19–28; Sacred Heart:
19:31–37; Christ the King: 18:33–37.

Year C, Trinity Sunday: 16:12–15.

6. Weekdays around Christmas

Advent, F in 3rd Week: 5:33–36.

December 31 to January 7: 1:1–2:12.

January 12: 3:22–30.

7. Weekdays in Lent

Week 4, M to Th: 4:43–5:47; F to S, 7:1–53.

Week 5, M to Th: 8:1–59; F: 10:31–42; S, 11:45–56.

Week 6, M: 12:1–11; T: 13:21–33, 36–38.

8. *Weekdays in Easter*

Week 1, T: 20:11–18; F: 21:1–14.

Week 2, M to Th: 3:1–36; F to S: 6:1–21.

Week 3, M to F: 6:22–69.

Week 4, M to T: 10:1–30; W: 12:44–50; Th: 13:16–30;
    F to S: 14:1–14.

Week 5, M to S: 14:21–15:21.

Week 6, M to S: 15:26–16:28.

Week 7, M to Th: 16:29–17:26; F to S: 20:15–25.

B. Johannine Texts for Sundays and Major Feasts

The annotations beside the texts (e.g. A 2 Lent) refer to the Year (A, B, C), the Sunday number (2, 3, 4, etc.), and the liturgical season (Advent, Lent, Easter, Ordinary Time).

1:1–18	ABC Christmas Day
1:6–8, 19–28	B 3 Advent
1:29–34	A 2 OT
1:35–42	B 2 OT
2:1–12	C 2 OT
2:13–25	B 3 Lent
3:14–21	B 4 Lent
3:16–18	A Trinity Sunday
4:5–42	A(BC) 3 Lent
6:1–15	B 17 OT
6:24–35	B 18 OT
6:41–51	B 19 OT
6:51–58	B 20 OT, A Corpus Christi

6:60–69	B 21 OT
7:37–39	ABC Vigil of Pentecost
8:1–11	C 5 Lent
9:1–41	A(BC) 4 Lent
10:1–10	A 4 Easter
10:11–18	B 4 Easter
10:27–30	C 4 Easter
11:1–45	A(BC) 5 Lent
12:20–33	B 5 Lent
12:12–16	B Palm Sunday
13:1–15	ABC Holy Thursday
13:31–33	C 5 Easter
14:1–12	A 5 Easter
14:15–21	A 6 Easter
14:23–29	C 6 Easter
15:1–8	B 5 Easter
15:9–17	B 6 Easter
16:12–15	C Trinity Sunday
17:1–11	A 7 Easter
17:11–19	B 7 Easter
17:20–26	C 7 Easter
18:1—19:42	ABC Good Friday
18:33–37	B. Christ the King
19:31–37	B Sacred Heart
20:1–9	ABC Easter
20:19–23	ABC Pentecost
20:19–31	ABC 2 Easter
21:1–19	C 3 Easter

For Further Reading

Ashton, John. *Understanding the Fourth Gospel.* Oxford. New York: Oxford University Press, 1991; 2nd ed., 2007.

Bauckham, Richard and C. Mosser, eds. *The Gospel of John and Christian Theology.* Grand Rapids: Eerdmans, 2008.

Brown, Raymond E. *The Gospel according to John.* The Anchor Yale Bible Commentaries. New York: Doubleday, 1966, 1970.

———. *The Community of the Beloved Disciple: The Lives, Loves and Hates of an Individual Church in New Testament Times.* New York: Paulist, 1979.

———. *An Introduction to the Gospel of John.* Edited by F. J. Moloney. New York: Doubleday, 2003.

Koester, Craig R. *The Word of Life: A Theology of John's Gospel.* Grand Rapids: Eerdmans, 2008.

Martyn, J. Louis. *History and Theology in the Fourth Gospel.* 3rd ed. Louisville: Westminster John Knox, 2003.

Moloney, Francis J. *The Gospel of John.* Sacra Pagina. Collegeville, MN: Liturgical Press, 1998.

Smith, Dwight M. *John. Abingdon New Testament Commentaries.* Nashville: Abingdon, 1999.

Stanley, David M. *"I Encountered God!" The Spiritual Exercises with the Gospel of John.* St. Louis: Institute of Jesuit Sources, 1986.

Thatcher, Thomas, ed. *What We Have Heard from the Beginning: The Past, Present, and Future of Johannine Studies.* Waco, TX: Baylor University Press, 2007.

Thatcher, Thomas and S. D. Moore, eds. *Anatomies of Narrative Criticism: The Past, Present, and Futures of the Fourth Gospel as Literature.* Atlanta: Society of Biblical Literature, 2008.

Thompson, Marianne M. *The God of the Gospel of John.* Grand Rapids: Eerdmans, 2001.

About the Author

Daniel J. Harrington, SJ, is professor of New Testament at Boston College School of Theology and Ministry. He wrote "The Word" column for *America* magazine from 2005 to 2008. He has been writing an annual survey of recent "Books on the Bible" for *America* since 1984. Harrington has been editor of *New Testament Abstracts* since 1972 and served as president of the Catholic Biblical Association in 1985–86. He was a member of the official team for editing the Dead Sea Scrolls and focused on the wisdom texts from Qumran. He is also the editor of the *Sacra Pagina* commentary on the New Testament (Liturgical Press) to which he contributed the volumes on Matthew, Mark (with John Donahue), and 1 & 2 Peter and Jude (with Donald Senior). He has published extensively on the New Testament and on Second Temple Judaism. He is the author of *Meeting St. Paul Today* (2008), *Meeting St. Luke Today* (2009), and *Meeting St. Matthew Today* (2010), all published by Loyola Press. His *Meeting St. Mark Today* is forthcoming.

Other books available in the *Meeting ... Today* series by Daniel J. Harrington, SJ

Meeting St. Matthew Today
$12.95 • 2914-5 • Paperback

Meeting St. Luke Today
$12.95 • 2916-9 • Paperback

Meeting St. Paul Today
$12.95 • 2734-9 • Paperback

All books in the *Meeting … Today* series by Daniel J. Harrington, SJ, are now available as Kindle and ePUB eBooks. Visit **www.loyolapress.com/harrington**, and click on the "other formats" tab to purchase these editions.

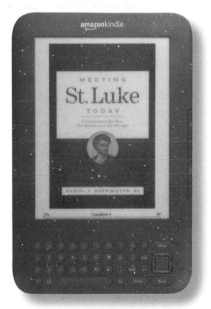

kindle ePUB

SpiritedTalk.org

WHERE YOUR IDEAS MATTER AND YOUR OPINIONS COUNT!

Do you have ideas and opinions to share with other leaders in the Catholic community, ideas and opinions that can shape the future of our faith?

If so, consider joining **www.spiritedtalk.org**, an online community of DREs, catechists, and other church leaders who participate in surveys and conversations on spiritual topics. Signing up is easy, and membership is FREE!

For more information about this opportunity to have your voice heard—and to hear what your peers are saying—visit **www.spiritedtalk.org** today!